I Wonder U

I Wonder U

How Prince Went beyond Race and Back

ADILIFU NAMA

Rutgers University Press

New Brunswick, Camden, and Newark, New Jersey, and London

Library of Congress Cataloging-in-Publication Data

Names: Nama, Adilifu, 1969- author.
Title: I wonder U: how Prince went beyond race and back / Adilifu Nama.
Description: New Brunswick : Rutgers University Press, 2019. | Includes
    bibliographical references and index.
Identifiers: LCCN 2019006593| ISBN 9781978805163 (pbk. : alk. paper) |
    ISBN 9781978805170 (hc-plc : alk. paper)
Subjects: LCSH: Prince—Criticism and interpretation. | Music and
    race—United States—History—20th century. | Sex in music—History—20th
    century.
Classification: LCC ML420.P974 N36 2019 | DDC 781.66092—dc23
LC record available at https://lccn.loc.gov/2019006593

A British Cataloging-in-Publication record for this book is available from the British Library.

www.rutgersuniversitypress.org

Manufactured in the United States of America

For my Pops, Art Nixon, who played Steely Dan, Rick James, and Pharoah Sanders loud enough for me to hear through my closed room door

Contents

I Wonder U

Introduction

Prince Rogers Nelson remains as enigmatic posthumously as he was when his career began. Such a state of unknowability is quite amazing given that we live in a world where overexposure is the norm and notoriety often eclipses talent and accomplishment. In today's TMZ media-saturated America virtually every tidbit of celebrity life, ranging from major events to personal bathroom habits, is fodder for attention. "Inquiring minds want to know," is the feeble justification for the continuous intrusion of our collective eyes into the lifestyles of the rich and famous. In stark contrast to our celebrity media millennium, where the private sphere appears near total obliteration, Prince has remained a mystery. Even with Prince's more unguarded moments in front of a camera he appeared keenly aware of the camera.[1] In physics it is called "the observer effect," whereby the act of observation changes the observed. As a consequence, the "real" Prince seemed perpetually shrouded in a performance of his own making.

As it stands, the established responses to piercing Prince's purple veil are the various unofficial biographies and "official" press packages that proclaim to reveal the real man behind the purple shroud. But all too often these revelations rely on culling anecdotes from former friends, band members, girlfriends, lovers, managers, bodyguards, and engineers who claim to have had a meaningful role, at one time or another, in Prince's personal or professional life. Throw in some sex and drugs and such stories become the basis of biographies that promise to reveal secret insights that titillate. But such facile attempts at revealing who Prince was are ultimately ineffective. Why? Because the abundant images and interviews of Prince demonstrate that Prince cannot be distilled to one basic version. Moreover, Prince's music, like the man himself, invites multiple interpretations.

On the one hand, songs like "Bambi" and "Let's Go Crazy" showcase brilliant guitar riffs that establish Prince as a rock music virtuoso. On the other hand, a track like "It's Gonna Be a Beautiful Night" underscores Prince as a practitioner of soulful dance music by melding James Brown percussiveness with the call-and-response of the black church. Risqué songs such as "Head," "Erotic City," and "Come" solidified Prince's status as a bona fide freaky-deeky regarding human sexuality, while bump-and-grind ballads like "International Lover" and "Do Me Baby" affirm Prince's self-proclaimed status as a sexy motherf***er. Then there is his groundbreaking first film *Purple Rain* (1984), a multitude of music videos, and the promotion of several subsequent films directed by Prince. Despite the prolific body of music, music videos, and films dictating the expansive boundaries of what makes Prince such a definitive figure, there remains one influential area that, at the least, is equal to defining Prince's larger-than-life status—race.

Without a doubt, when it comes to popular music and race in America, reductive terms such as "race records," "race music," "black music," "rhythm and blues," and "urban music" have all had a turn circumscribing, more so than describing, the type of music made and the audience expected to listen to it. Admittedly, music has no color, but that does not mean American pop music is not fundamental in contributing to the construction of racial notions of blackness and black racial formation in America. Prince's meaning, place, and contribution to American pop culture increase in magnitude when measured against this backdrop, a recording industry with a long, dubious record and reputation for dictating how black artists are positioned, viewed, and marketed.

Prince challenged and periodically subverted established racial notions for how popular blackness was imagined, promoted, and circulated in U.S. society by combining image and sound, style and substance, politics and pleasure with blatant self-promotion. Surprisingly, and for the most part, the discussion around the production, consumption, and meaning of Prince has steered clear of these meta-issues of race in America, even though Prince's career offers the opportunity to examine the racial fault lines that run deep and long in the American music industry and American pop culture. For the most part, the assortment of books on Prince has revolved around him as a celebrity and the lifestyle his star celebrity permitted. Accordingly, the analysis of Prince has trodden on the well-worn territory of the unauthorized biography. Furthermore, because of Prince's reputation and practice of "letting the music speak" for him, conventional biographies have overwhelmingly relied on personal anecdotes. Almost any person that has interacted with Prince is used to provide some anecdote to derive clues concerning Prince's personality and beliefs. The purely biographical approach, however, fails to fully chart and provide critical insights concerning how Prince successfully subverted the tendency to be marginalized in the recording industry as a "black" musician that plays "black" music. Whereas a multitude of black musicians and performers remained ensconced in the informal racial colloquium of being a "black superstar," Prince, or more accurately the image of Prince, eluded such classification. *I Wonder U* is about examining how and answering why this is the case.

The central theme of *I Wonder U* rests on revealing and deconstructing the shifting contours of the racial dynamics that worked to construct Prince as both black and not black. Moreover, *I Wonder U* brings to light the historical, ongoing, and highly combustible racial politics in pop music and the broader cultural politics of race in America by exploring the weaknesses and strengths, regressive and progressive tendencies, racial misfires and successes embodied by Prince Rogers Nelson. By examining Prince Rogers Nelson's self-invention this book critically illuminates the racial politics of the American music industry, pop culture, and modes of racial meaning circulating in American society. In doing so, *I Wonder U* explains how Prince articulated and symbolized racial blackness in a manner that challenged and subverted established racial notions for how popular blackness is imagined, promoted, and circulated in U.S. society vis-à-vis his use of cross-dressing, vulgar sexuality, romanticism, homoerotic fantasy, lies, musical innovations, and audacious showmanship.

I Wonder U takes Prince's public image and performances and places them in critical dialogue with long-standing racial discourses, debates, and emerging trends concerning black racial formation in America. Moreover, this type of "racial reading" involves a comparative historical contextualization of Prince to uncover potential points of cause and effect/affect concerning the racial politics Prince represented and the various modes of mediated blackness Prince symbolized. Ultimately, Prince's career is a mirror in which to view the racial expectations, racial imagination, and fluctuations in the popular expression of blackness operating in American popular culture across several historical eras.

I Wonder U adopts the tone of a cultural critic and the intellectual posture of a critical theorist to articulate a straightforward take on the mediation of Prince's blackness, the various modes of mediation deployed, and the ways in which this mediation challenged, subverted, or reinforced a broader racial discourse in American society. As such, the style of this book is openly indebted to Leroi Jones's (Amiri Baraka) *Blues People* (1963), a seminal articulation of the social and anthropological significance of black music and its relationship to black racial formation in America. Yet the intellectual pitch of this project is informed by the racial and cultural deconstruction of black music found in the work of Ben Sidran, Greg Tate, Mark Anthony Neal, Nelson George, Stanley Crouch, Guthrie Ramsey Jr., Rickey Vincent, and the excellent social commentary woven into James McBride's take on James Brown. These accomplished intellectuals and critics have all provided clarity and coherence to the intersection of race and a variety of black music idioms from jazz, R&B, and funk to soul and hip-hop.

For Prince, the majority of scholarship and cultural criticism concerning race is discussed as a subtext rather than as a cornerstone for the construction and deconstruction of Prince in American popular culture. For example, the book *Prince: Inside the Music and the Masks* (2011) by Ronin Ro is a rigorous journalistic report on Prince's music career. The book delves deep into Prince's prolific body of work and culls copious amounts of information from a range of articles and interviews with professional associates and personal contacts. Ro even takes on the issue of race with his provocatively titled chapter "Don't Make Me Black," a quote, attributed to Prince early in his career, spoken to a music executive as he prepared to finish recording his first album for Warner Brothers Records.[2] Prince's racial request is loaded with implications and a bundle of questions. Does Prince's statement mean he does not identify as a black person? Is Prince self-hating? Disappointingly, neither the chapter nor the book goes beyond reporting what Prince supposedly said.

Prince's statement also raises psychological and personality-driven questions that speak to the inner machinations of his mind. Admittedly, expecting a book to pry open and peer inside the mind of Prince to ascertain his true motivations and goals is unreasonable. But at that other side of the continuum that includes Prince's "Don't make me black" request are real issues concerning the history of Jim Crow and how the American record industry is rooted in the racial reality of the American body politic. Prince's edict also suggests that black racial identity is something that is "made," which is to say produced, assembled, and constructed. Surprisingly, and for the most part, the discussion around the production, consumption, and meaning of popular blackness concerning Prince has avoided these meta-issues of race in America.

Only Touré's book *I Would Die 4 U: Why Prince Became an Icon* (2013) and Ben Greenman's *Dig If You Will the Picture* (2017) examine the relationship between the American racial milieu and Prince's ascendency to iconic status. There are flashes of critical insight for Touré, a cultural critic who has shown considerable writing chops when race has been a contested cornerstone of debate. Unfortunately, Touré's take on Prince only makes minor incursions into the ideological thicket of black racial formation in America. Overall, the book reads more as an admiring love letter than a critical treatise on the social and cultural racial dynamics that dovetailed with the marketing of Prince to America's music-buying public.

In contrast, Greenman casts a broader sociocultural net than Touré in chronicling the various permutations of Prince over several decades. Greenman's analysis, however, is often hampered by a haphazard presentation of information. He slips back and forth from one decade to the next, like a wayward time traveler, rushing from one pivotal event only to abandon it for some minuscule moment that promises to shed a fresh perspective on a particular Prince song. The result, at best, is a mixed bag. To their credit, both Touré and Greenman engage the racial politics of the recording industry and American popular culture but neither author sustains a racial critique nor reveals the deep connections and import of race on the image of Prince.

For the most part, any prolonged analysis of Prince waded into the creative process and conditions under which Prince's music was created. For example, *Prince and the Purple Rain Studio Sessions* (2017) is a detailed tome concerned most with the confines of the studio and minutia related to the music. Alan Light's *Let's Go Crazy: The Making of Purple Rain* (2014) is exclusively built around examining Prince at the height of his commercial popularity. As a consequence, Light's book casts dim illumination on any other aspect of Prince's social and political symbolism not tied to *Purple Rain* the film or the soundtrack. In addition, Matt Thorne's *Prince* (2012) delves deep into Prince's prolific body of work but offers only periodic insights concerning the racial hurdles Prince faced. Armand White's *New*

Position: The Prince Chronicles (2016) is a compendium of White's previous essays and reviews of Prince. On the one hand, White is a trenchant critic and makes astute observations about Prince and the racial backdrop he operates in for most of his career. On the other hand, White's essays are drawn from past publications, making his crisp commentary more of a snapshot of the moment that frequently sounds dated.

One of the most sustained analyses of the socially constructed nature and impact of Prince's image concerns gender. The book *Prince: The Making of a Pop Music Phenomenon* (2011) uses gender, in general, and queerness, in particular, as the dual image platforms to explore what the authors coined "the Prince experience" and the "Princian effect." Unfortunately, the clunky nomenclature deployed to frame how Prince challenged traditional gender norms and provided a range of innovative styles of stage performativity turns into mind-numbing academic prose and farfetched analysis. For example, the authors compare Prince to Malcolm X and argue, "Prince has shirked categorization according to ethnicity, gender and sexuality. Like Malcolm X, Prince has embodied a rejection of being pigeonholed, arguably a mechanism of liberation from the chains of white patriarchy. In fact, he is one of the few black pop artists who have dared speak the truth about masculinity and the politics of essentialization. And he has done this by articulating his look as much as his music. Such self-acceptance leads to a consideration of what it is to be 'cool.'"[3] Given this odd comparison, I'm not sure which one of these iconic figures the authors have misunderstood more, Malcolm X or Prince? Either way, despite a variety of interesting observations and conclusions concerning gender, the accuracy of their conclusions concerning how race relates to the image and music of Prince is questionable.

In contrast to all of these works, *I Wonder U* is committed to situating Prince in the matrix of racial meaning and discourse circulating in U.S. society, the music industry, black culture, and American pop culture. Prince's racial misdirects and misfires deserve prolonged critical scrutiny and deconstruction to reveal the range of racial meaning imbedded in the visual signifiers Prince marshaled to create and (re)produce an image of himself for popular consumption. Consequently, when one is examining the topic of Prince's music, image plays a significant part in determining the racial meaning of the music and the musician, an approach that also requires a deconstruction of the stagecraft created and used to construct his persona and propel his career.

The bulk of discussions around Prince rightfully place his emergence in conjunction with the emergence of the music video and the beginning of MTV as a music-image-producing medium. John Mundy's book *Popular Music On Screen: From Hollywood Musical to Music Video* (1999) and Murray Forman's *One Night on TV Is Worth Weeks at the Paramount: Popular Music on Early Television* (2012) stand out as exemplary bookends that reveal the relationship between pop music and television/cinema. Both examine the relationship between music and image and are primarily concerned with the political economy of production and the ideological fallout concerning commodification. Mundy's work, in particular, consolidates television and cinema under the category of "the screen" to discuss the image focused aspect of music. Here musical performance is privileged along with various broadcast conventions that speak to particular industry-centered aesthetic innovations along with the evolution of music programming. Ironically, the visually dominated mediums of television and to a lesser extent film have played a dramatic role in the music industry. The debut of Music Television (MTV) in 1981 caused video airplay to displace the centrality of radio airplay.[4] This radical disruption soon became a cornerstone for promotion and consumption of music.

Forman's work is also a conceptual touchstone in that he raises the intersectional issue of race, music, and television in his book and underscores the importance of the racialized image of music on television to challenge dominant racial discourses. The takeaway from both books is that the look of music, in this case, the screen image of pop music, is central to its marketing and meaning, a conceptual point of departure for this book's examination of Prince. Accordingly, this book focuses on the album cover and inside art, televisual music video image, and cinematic persona Prince presented to the public as the point of analysis, not merely personal anecdotes to deconstruct how Prince negotiated and what he signified about racial blackness.

Chapter 1, "Incognegro," examines the factors and context contributing to Prince establishing a stage persona outside of established R&B representations of black culture and style. In particular, this chapter examines how Prince challenged conventional notions of black popular masculinity by drawing from traditional rock and roll tropes, punk rock, and the emergent post-punk genre of new wave. Prince's mash-up of these music genres is covered and examined for how it not only provided the groundwork for the establishment of the "Minneapolis Sound" but also bridged racial distinctions vis-à-vis Prince's musical innovation(s). Particular attention is also given to the intraracial tensions and optics concerning the representation of popular black masculinity symbolized by the professional and personal rivalry between Prince and Rick James, Prince's first music and ideological adversary regarding racial representation.

The second chapter, "On the Black Hand Side," examines how Prince gave rise to various creative outlets to release "black" music geared to a black audience. Particular attention is given to The Time, one of Prince's most definitive sonic articulations of blackness, and the lingerie-clad girl group Vanity 6. Prince was responsible for creating and making the music for both groups. The chapter also examines the retrograde racial politics of MTV programming and provides a solid foundation for understanding how and why Prince's eventual mainstream breakthrough, in contrast to that of Rick James, evolved into a division that came to represent a sharp racial rift, as well as underscores the ideological stakes and sociocultural import of MTV's racially discriminatory video programming during the 1980s.

Chapter 3, "Enfant Terrible," analyzes the auspicious mainstream superstar success Prince achieved from the crossover film sensation *Purple Rain* (1984). The semibiographical film was a crossover coup and marked the pinnacle of Prince's pop formula achievement. The racial symbolism circulating in *Purple Rain* is deconstructed alongside long-standing debates concerning black representation in the Hollywood film industry. The chapter also maps the outer limits of Prince's crossover pop music and image formula with the release of *Around the World in a Day* (1985) and the multiple signifiers Prince invoked with his shifting image.

In chapter 4, "Cherry Bomb," the Prince-directed film *Under the Cherry Moon* (1986) is interrogated for how the film registers multiple anxieties concerning black racial identity, crossover success, white privilege, and black heterosexual masculinity. Despite the film being a box office flop the movie stands as a stinging indictment of whiteness along class and cultural lines. Chapter 4 charts these tensions and Prince's conscious turn to a black aesthetic, a development fully confronted in Prince's concert film *Sign O' the Times* (1987) and surprising withdrawal of *The Black Album* (1987) just prior to its scheduled release. Chapter 4 appraises the strength and weaknesses of these respective projects for how they engaged black style and reaffirmed Prince as a "black" artist that made "black" music.

Chapter 5, "Chaos and Crossroads," examines Prince's 1990s struggle to maintain relevancy in the face of hip-hop after a protracted attempt to dismiss hip-hop and his abrupt about-face with the genre, as a dominant and popular form of black expression. The chapter also examines how Prince-like artists, such as D'Angelo, emerged to fulfill the nostalgic impulse for Prince music rooted more in R&B than in unconvincing articulations of hip-hop and underscores the similarities between Prince and Miles Davis as sonic visionaries. The chapter concludes with a discussion of the cultural work *The Dave Chappelle* show performed to humanize and reaffirm Prince's "blackness" in our collective popular consciousness, along with the short-comings and successes of Prince's relationship to hip-hop.

Chapter 6, "Don't Call It a Comeback," covers Prince moving away from his signature sex junkie image and sex-infused songs. The chapter further details Prince cementing his status as a racially transcendent entertainer in American popular culture yet simultaneously asserting a black political sensibility through performativity, personal style, and protest. Lastly, the chapter charts the various ways Prince performed cultural work around race and the modes of mediated blackness Prince reconfigured and adopted in relationship to racial dynamics found in American popular culture. In this manner, chapter 6 engages discourse concerning how music marks the vicissitudes of race in America and how Prince used it to express racial protest.

The final chapter, "Dearly Beloved: An Epitaph," examines the interplay between popular memory and racial identity for framing how Prince is collectively remembered and celebrated. The politics and power to define Prince's racial politics and, in most instances the erasure of his blackness, take center stage. The chapter also includes a personal reflection on the meaning and legacy of Prince as a racial shape-shifter.

Without a doubt, Prince was a musical genius and innovator, but he also challenged and periodically subverted established racial notions for how popular blackness was imagined, promoted, and circulated in U.S. society. In so doing, Prince became an iconic and often racially transcendent figure. Nonetheless, even if it was not readily recognized, Prince stood in critical dialogue with long-standing racial discourses, debates, and emerging trends concerning black racial formation in America. *I Wonder U: How Prince Went Beyond Race and Back* brings to light this progression in pop music and American society by exploring the weaknesses and successes embodied by Prince Rogers Nelson.

1

Incognegro

> Pino: *It's different. Magic, Eddie,*
> **PRINCE** . . . *are not niggers. I mean,*
> *they're not black, I mean—let me*
> *explain myself. They're—they're not*
> *really black. I mean, they're black, but*
> *they're not really black. They're more*
> *than black. It's different.*
> —Dialogue from *Do the Right Thing*
> (1989)

> Now where I come from / We don't let
> society tell us how it's supposed to be /
> Our clothes, our hair, we don't care / it's
> all about being there . . .
> —Prince, "Uptown" (1980)

Official records declare that Prince Rogers Nelson was the son of Mattie Shaw and John L. Nelson and was born June 7, 1958, in Minneapolis, Minnesota. I would place the date closer to January 26, 1980, in Los Angeles, California, on a television show called *American Bandstand* (1952–1989), a program that featured teenagers and young adults dancing to the middle-of-the-road pop hits of the time. Situated between our imagination and Prince's self-invention rest the music and myth of Prince, an image first presented to mainstream America on *American Bandstand*. In this sense, the public imagination, as much as his mother and father, created Prince, and the television studio, as much the hospital, marks the venue for where Prince was born.

On *American Bandstand* Prince played a truncated version of his hit single "I Wanna Be Your Lover," off his self-titled second album, *Prince* (1979). Prince had written and played every instrument for every song, but for his performance on the television show Prince brought a band. Dez Dickerson and André Cymone played guitars. Buried in the backdrop, behind the drum set, were Bobby Z and, off to the side, Gayle Chapman, who stood behind her keyboard, a shadowy silhouette that swayed back and forth in the background. Matt Fink was on the synthesizer dressed in a striped prison inmate outfit. Prince stood out front wearing formfitting gold lamé pants, a matching pair of low-cut boots, and an oversized, long-sleeved top unbuttoned down to the navel (more of a woman's blouse than a man's shirt), a look that literally promoted navel gazing. After Prince concluded performing, Dick Clark, the maestro of mainstream pop music and host of the show, rushed over to engage Prince and the band in some light banter.

Clark seemed stunned to have heard that such a funky hook–driven midtempo groove was crafted and perfected in Upper Midwest America. He asked Prince, "How did you learn how to do this in Minneapolis? This is not the kind of music that comes from Minneapolis, Minnesota." Perhaps Clark's sense of genuine amazement was misinterpreted by Prince as a slight against Prince's hometown, or maybe Prince froze, like a doe-eyed deer, staring into the bright klieg lights of fame. Either way, Prince responded to Clark's succession of questions with one-word responses and a string of odd mannerisms. At first, Prince appears genuinely embarrassed, then obstinate, and by the end, Prince looks like he is flirting with Clark and daring Clark not to kiss him right on the stage. Not surprisingly, Prince's *American Bandstand* interview acquired varying degrees of lore over the decades as another Prince-created ploy to make a very routine and perfunctory part of a show memorable to those who witnessed it and talked about by those who missed it.[1]

This national introduction of Prince to America and the mysterious and strange demeanor of the interviewee would define Prince's persona for years to come, a mystery wrapped inside a riddle at the center of a maze. In retrospect, Clark's confusion over the sound and geographical origin of Prince's music is not that incredible given the conventional wisdom that Minneapolis, Minnesota, does not fit the profile or pattern of various chocolate cities as an epicenter for a specific form of black popular music, cultural expression, and sonic innovation.[2] For the most part, the migration of millions of African Americans fleeing the stifling racism of the rural South, and/or spurred by the pull of industrial labor opportunities in northeastern cities between the early 1900s and the 1960s, set in place a dramatic increase of black populations in northeastern, midwestern, and western metropolitan areas. These budding black urban communities remixed the soundtrack of rural southern black life, the blues (born of black enslavement and Jim Crow segregation), into signature sonic styles that beget new forms of black music associated with geographically specific places. Chicago begot Chicago blues, and later Chicago house music. New York birthed bebop, straight-ahead jazz, and later hip-hop. Detroit originated the Motown sound and Detroit techno. Dayton, Ohio, furnished the funk, while the Philly soul sound of Kenneth Gamble and Leon Huff kept America dancing in the mid-1970s and Washington, D.C., popularized the polyrhythms of go-go. Although not exhaustive, these are all notable examples of how particular concentrated black geographical regions are synonymous with a particular form of black music associated with significant black populations in particular urban spaces. According to the 1970 census, just ten years prior to Prince's debut on *American Bandstand*, Minnesota's population was 98 percent Caucasian.

At first blush the statistical facts appear to support Dick Clark's stunned statement of disbelief about the geographical birthplace of Prince's funky pop dance ditty. Common sense dictated that Minneapolis, Minnesota, was too white and too square for anything black and hip to emerge. Moreover, before Prince, the most notable musician from the "Land of 10,000 Lakes" was the popular white folk artist Bob Dylan, a suitable match for the prairie lands and pioneer spirit of Minnesota. Perhaps Clark could only recall how Minneapolis was the setting for the groundbreaking but virtually all-white *Mary Tyler Moore Show* (1970–1977). As a result, Clark's stunned reaction seems quite reasonable after his having seen three black men fronting a multiracial band from Minnesota, crooning about unrequited sexual desire over a lean, bluesy, bass hook–laden track. Nevertheless, black racial formation dynamics did impact Minneapolis, Minnesota, in such a way as to shape a particular soundscape.[3]

Purple Snow, a minibook-length liner note analysis for a two-disc set compilation of demos and one-off releases of local Minneapolis black bands, chronicles the racial dynamics of the Minneapolis music scene, up to and around the breakout music success of Prince. The liner notes are a tour de force for matching names, faces, places, and venues with musical output and capture the social alchemy of the Minneapolis music scene covering a ten-year period from 1972 until early 1982. The extraordinary exposé covers the truncated experience of notable local bands, the unfulfilled potential of remarkable talent, the Rubik's Cube–like configurations of band personnel that played together and details a litany of false starts and musical dreams denied and deferred before Prince became a singular musical force. Most importantly, *Purple Snow*'s liner notes reveal that the bandstand and the dance floor were contested spaces in Minneapolis when it came to racial issues. In Minneapolis black bands needed to include a few white (or at least white looking) members to get booked for a gig, a recurring subtext touched on by several musicians in the book.[4] For the Minneapolis music scene white inclusion in a black enterprise was necessary for a black band to gain employment. This regional quirk was in stark contrast to the general Black Power on wax era that overlapped with the Minneapolis music scene covered in *Purple Snow*.

Black Power politics began in the mid-1960s and by 1972 had reached mainstream pop status when *Rolling Stone* magazine, a premier music periodical, placed Huey P. Newton, the cofounder of the Black Panther Party, on its cover. Although, by the early 1970s, the Black Power movement was waning as a presence in the halls of political power the black revolution was making its mark in the ranks of R&B and soul music. In fact, during this brief period several successful black artists became troubadours of black pride and black cultural awareness. Songs such as the Impressions' "We're a Winner" (1968), James Brown's "Say It Loud, I'm Black and I'm Proud" (1969), and Marvin Gaye's "What's Going On" (1971) raised a range of racial and urban issues Black Power advocates had previously voiced concern over. Concept albums like Aretha Franklin's *Young, Gifted and Black* (1972), Stevie Wonder's *Innervision* (1973), and to a lesser extent Curtis Mayfield's *Superfly* (1972) also tackled the challenges and triumphs of the black experience.[5] Even jazz giant Miles Davis released *On the Corner* (1972), a fusion-funk experimental album designed to reach black youth. Consequently, for the Minneapolis music scene, the inclusion of whites in black music projects was strikingly out of step with the political and cultural trends informing early to mid-1970s black music. It would take the rise of disco music in the mid-1970s to blunt the strident racial politics of Black Power on the bandstand and dance floor.

By 1976 not only did a variety of disco bands include white members, a white band named Wild Cherry even endeared themselves to black audiences with the disco hit "Play that Funky Music (white boy)." With disco the political imprint found in the sophisticated sonic constructions of Marvin Gaye, Stevie Wonder, James Brown, and Curtis Mayfield faded away to the pulse of monotonous beats and brain-dead lyrics. Across dance floors, from New York to Los Angeles, disco music was a rhythmic diatribe that perfectly fit the frenetic domain of clubs like Studio 54, where the combination of cocaine and a driving beat helped unleash repressed sexual energy and marshaled the latent hedonistic excesses of young Americans on the make. By 1978, the year Prince released his first album, titled *For You*, disco dominated the airwaves and the type of overt black racial and social awareness present in R&B during the early to mid-1970s was, for the most part, abandoned.

As a Minneapolis native Prince developed in a black music scene where whiteness was not displaced, and with *For You*, like the disco sensibility of the period, white band members had a prominent place in Prince's plans for his first touring band.[6] In terms of his sound, Prince did deviate from the disco craze sweeping across the recording industry and the American pop landscape. *For You* rejected the blaring horns and driving disco beats that dominated the dance floors and commercial radio of the time. *For You* was a midtempo, ballad-laden LP, a collection of syrupy sweet melodies and falsetto pining over lost lovers and fledgling declarations of devotion. The lyrics sounded like mediocre poetry delivered with all the sincerity found in a high school teenager's love letters. Although the vulnerability Prince shared on the various tracks was convincing, without a doubt, the most compelling element of Prince's debut was the musicianship (Prince wrote, played, and produced nearly all the music).

For You contained tracks with multiple bridges, breaks, and so many tempo shifts that the release bordered on a manic display of musical virtuosity. Rather than an album that offered one signature sound, *For You* was a sonic smorgasbord. The variety of changes, just on one track alone, demonstrated Prince was a very talented but unsure musician searching for a sound, afraid to commit to a singular groove. The track "My Love Is Forever" displayed not just versatility but also a preview of how Prince could construct beautiful arrangements and seamlessly incorporate rock-styled guitar solos, a preview of the type of genre-shattering musicianship that later becomes a signature element of his sound. "My Love Is Forever" also signaled that Prince was an artist who not only went against the grain but also had the musical mechanics to make hook-centric hits, a point most clearly articulated with the song "Soft and Wet," a modest hit single on the *For You* release. "Soft and Wet," was the standout track on the LP and almost cracked the top ten of *Billboard* R&B singles with its #12 ranking. Most importantly, "Soft and Wet," demonstrated Prince could construct an upbeat and tightly arranged pop tune that resonated with a black music-buying public. But too many tracks like "As Long as We're Together," "Baby," "So Blue," and "I'm Yours" sounded as fresh as two-day-old doughnuts.

In the final analysis, *For You* was a release that *promised* something big rather than *being* something big. But just as important as the music on the *For You* LP was for marking Prince's sonic potential the cover image of the LP is central to evaluating the racial politics Prince represented. Admittedly, the status of the cover image/art of an album has significantly diminished in our download and digital age of music consumption. All the same, before the dramatic shift in the distribution and purchasing of music, the cover art of a new release for a new artist was a cornerstone feature of the overall music project.[7] Music scholar Evan Eisenberg makes this astute analysis concerning the significance of the cover LP image: "Every mode of record listening leaves us with a need for something, if not someone, to see and touch. The adoration of the disc itself is one response (though this, as we have seen, answers other needs as well). But as records tend to look alike and one doesn't want fingerprints on them, in practice one adores the album cover, and this impulse (together with the science of marketing) is behind the importance of cover design in the record business." Certainly, the music from *For You* was the centerpiece of Prince's debut album. Yet, given Eisenberg's conceptual framing, reason also dictates the cover image of Prince's first release was of paramount significance. Consequently, the cover art image of the *For You* LP is a significant source of meaning and image construction because it marks the beginning of the various modes of black racial identity Prince adopted in the wake of his first release. What does the *For You* cover convey about Prince? Interestingly, both the cover and the photographs inside work intensely to promote Prince as an ethereal, otherworldly entity.

The front cover consists of a headshot of Prince sporting an oversized Afro filling the frame and eerily backlit. Prince's head is placed slightly off-centered, and his eyes are askance yet peering forward, as if daring the observer to make direct eye contact and stare back at him. The confrontational characteristic of the pose is somewhat subverted by photographic special effects. Light trails streak across the picture, creating a dissonant illusion of movement, a head in motion that is motionless. The only other image of Prince related to the LP is found on the inside LP sleeve jacket. The photo on the inside sleeve has three identical pictures of a nude Prince sitting beside himself on a bed hovering in space. Prince is holding a guitar strategically placed to block his genitals. A less adventurous reading of the reproduction of three exact images of Prince positioned next to the other is that the manipulated photograph denotes the multiple roles Prince had in creating, writing, and producing the album. Both the "blurred movement" headshot and the image of Prince sitting on a floating bed marked a literal decontextualization of Prince and signified he was a figure that transcends time and geography (Prince is literally floating in space sitting on a bed!). Despite these mediated artistic productions the *For You* pictures may arguably be the most honest representations of Prince.

Ronin Ro, in the rigorously detailed book *Prince: Inside the Music and the Masks* (2011), asserts that Prince rejected having an art director for the cover and decided to just pose for photographer Joe Giannetti. In my email correspondence with Joe Giannetti he recounts the photo shoots and highlights the tension between industry practices and the "as-is" aesthetic Prince embodied on *For You*:

> I was contacted by an art director by the name of Jeff Fermarkus his client was Prince's manager at the time his name was Owen Hussey. Contrary to the normal method of operating there was no pre-planning involved in how to go about photographing Prince. I was not privy to any reason that we did not have a preplanning meeting but I was used to a lot of art directors functioning by the "seat-of-the-pants" so to speak. Prince arrived 2 P.M. with several of his friends and he was sporting a [sic] Afro haircut. After a discussion with Owen and Jeff and myself I expressed my slight concern about the Afro haircut because my impression was that it was getting somewhat out of date on the West and East coast as a fashion look.

My creative dilemma was that there were no makeup artists at that time in Minneapolis that really knew how to do makeup for a person of color. The second dilemma was that they wanted a dark background; my assumption is they wanted his face to stand out. I noticed that Prince had a two-day stubble. The style of the shot "blurred movement" was not used much at the time and would be eye catching. In retrospect I would have to say that their idea of permitting him to have a [sic] Afro haircut at that time was their desire not to upset the apple cart or Prince's feelings and they didn't have any other solution nor the desire to try and sell it to Prince.

Later on I was also asked to do the inside sleeve and pictures for that album. They had decided to photograph him on a circular bed with a round half circle window behind [him]. He wanted to be photographed nude sitting on the edge of the bed playing the guitar. I remember calling the art director at Warner Bros. and explaining this shot that Prince had desired, I have no recollection whether his manager at the time also wanted it. We had the same situation with the makeup artist, but in San Francisco, the makeup artist knew just exactly how to put the makeup on Prince's face.

Buried in Joe Giannetti's recollection of events surrounding the *For You* album photo shoot is how race was a background but significant presence prescribing the terms of Prince's introduction to the world. Because of a lack of professional makeup artists with experience and knowhow working with black folk for the *For You* album photo shoot, Prince, for all intents and purposes, presents a naturalistic and unadorned picture of himself for the public to consume.

Clearly, the inside album sleeve signaled an austere thematic with the photo of Prince sitting in the nude strumming his guitar. The nudity is obviously meant to evoke vulnerability and sincerity as an artist, a visual affect that Prince would also repeat on later albums. But most importantly, on the cover of *For You*, Prince's blowout Afro hairstyle and light brown complexion foreground his racial identity. Although the content of Prince's debut release failed to offer any overt articulations concerning blackness, his image revealed traces of the popular cultural imprint the Black Power movement had had on fashion during the Black Power era of the late 1960s—the Afro.

No other black hairstyle has visually symbolized a self-conscious rejection of aesthetic notions of white superiority, affirmed black racial pride, and signified militant racial politics than the Afro. The blaxploitation film genre of the early 1970s provided numerous films that used the oversized Afro as visual shorthand to convey the political sensibility of an assortment of cardboard and stereotypical characters. Despite the Afro increasing in popularity and size, the hairstyle was diminishing in political symbolism; a variety of celebrities, popular sports figures and performers adopted an oversized Afro as a cornerstone of their "look," not as a signifier of their racial politics. Case in point, Bob Ross, PBS's favorite draw-along-art-instructor, sported a large Afro for years on his show, *The Joy of Painting* (1983–1994). His Afro became such a signature and iconic part of his image the hairstyle crystallized his personal style and, arguably, eclipsed the educational content and artistic raison d'être of the show. And he was a white man.

Correspondingly, in his account of the *For You* photo shoot, Giannetti underscores, how Prince's Afro was already a "dated" style, circa 1978, when Prince shows up to take pictures for the album. Although, the Afro was greatly diminished as a signifier of Black Power militancy by the late 1970s, the hairstyle still remained a powerful sign of black racial identity rooted in black cultural history and social memory. While an array of black hairstyles, such as braids, curly perms, dreadlocks, cornrows, fades, the quo vadis, and even Jheri curls, have all vied for space as the most relevant symbolic syntax of racial identity in America the Afro has endured as a signifier of a distinctive cultural cue of a black racial identity throughout Black America.[8] Admittedly, the Afro that Prince rocked on the cover of *For You* was not able to fully signify the politicized racial pride of the recent past or the urban dandyism popularized in blaxploitation cinema, but it is an image born of and indebted to Black Power. In this sense, the *For You* cover stands in stark contrast to Prince's second studio album, the self-titled *Prince* (1979).

The success of *Prince* made *For You* such an unfamiliar release that the latter album's most significant impact might be as a bonus question in a game of trivial pursuit. On his second release, along with subsequent promotional materials for the album, Prince dramatically veered away from any readily recognizable vestiges of Black Power racial representation found on *For You*. Admittedly, the *Prince* album cover did share a similar motif with the front of the *For You* album, Prince staring blankly into the camera. Except the former presented Prince significantly exposing his bare torso, his copper tone complexion juxtaposed against a baby blue background and sporting a chemically straightened perm meant to mimic white hair texture. The chemically straightened hairstyle Prince wore clearly signaled he was launching a new look, a fluffy Farrah Fawcett–like perm. In actuality, Prince mined retrograde notions of black representation with his striking hairstyle. African American men chemically straightening their hair has a long-standing history going back to the 1920s, but the style came of age in the 1950s with black male entertainers straightening their hair (e.g., Little Richard, Chuck Berry, James Brown, Nat King Cole, Sammy Davis Jr., Jackie Wilson, and Miles Dewy Davis).[9] By the late 1960s, however, and in the wake of the Black Power movement, the people most associated with having chemically relaxed hair were self-hating blacks, black street pimps, the black rock musician Jimi Hendrix, and Ron O' Neal, an antihero protagonist in the film *Superfly* (1972).

Against this historical backdrop, Prince's "processed" hair and nude torso album photo cover made him look more eccentric than fashionable, an image that clearly signaled Prince was distinct from the sophisticated blackness represented by popular R&B groups in the late 1970s and early 1980s. For example, the black dance music group Chic dressed in smart business attire on their album cover for *C'est Chic* (1978). Their look epitomized the stylish upward mobility of black bourgeois materialism of the late 1970s. Similarly, Michael Jackson, on the cover of his *Off the Wall* (1979) LP, was a model of black ultra-hip sophistication when he wore a tuxedo and black bowtie. In the late 1970s and early 1980s, such imagery symbolically dovetailed with the real economic success stories of the black professional strivers that experienced unprecedented expansion into the American workplace as the first-wave beneficiaries of affirmative action.[10]

In contrast to the sophisticated symbolism of black upward social mobility, economic pride and success presented on album covers such as Diana Ross's *Baby It's Me* (1977), The Gap Band's *The Gap Band III* (1980), and the Brothers Johnson's *Winners* (1981) Prince mined prior black stylistic conventions that were culturally shunned, at the time, and adopted unconventional imagery. For example, the back of the *Prince* album depicted Prince nude and riding a white horse with wings. By reproducing the image of Prince riding an enchanted equine the image signified the rider was also otherworldly and possessed mystical qualities. Accordingly, the back album cover affirmed Prince as a figure that defies conventional categorization. But it would take more than a retro-hairstyle and a white horse with wings to unmoor Prince's pop image from totalizing notions of a black racial identity given how the breakout single from the *Prince* album, "I Wanna Be Your Lover," stood firm for two weeks on the black R&B music charts as a number one song and helped propel the album to number three on the Top

"I Wanna Be Your Lover" (1980) video still

Album R&B chart. On the whole, the sound and style of "I Wanna Be Your Lover," was fairly straightforward and affirmed a conventional rootedness in black culture. In contrast, the television performances and music videos for "I Wanna Be Your Lover," mark, in earnest, the establishment of Prince as a racially subversive figure and sexual shape shifter. Even though Prince's very first television performance announced he was far different from any black pop idol or traditional R&B performer, like Prince's first album, his television premiere was, for the most part, an obscure affair.

Prince made his television premiere on Burt Sugarman's *The Midnight Special* (1972–1981), an early-morning, ninety-minute musical variety show that featured a wide variety of bands, musicians, and entertainers, both established and new. By today's standards *The Midnight Special* is an obscure reference at best, but in retrospect, it was an innovative show.[11] *The Midnight Special* was unabashedly edgy, a point accentuated by the vocal antics of Wolfman Jack, the show's wild-eyed announcer. The list of guest performers on *The Midnight Special* was a Who's Who list of bad boy performers such as Richard Pryor, Monty Python, Steve Martin, Redd Foxx, Freddie Prinze, and George Carlin. Accordingly, by the time Prince hit *The Midnight Special* stage on January 12, 1980, he was well within the tradition of the television show's tendency of airing provocative performers, and on that theme, Prince did not disappoint. Prince, in a gender-bending outfit consisting of black leggings, black-heeled boots, and zebra-striped panties, preened and pranced around the stage pleading to the audience in his signature falsetto, "I Wanna Be Your Lover."

Historically, the black queer performer, at best, was often seen as a novelty act and marginalized in relationship to mainstream black R&B performers and groups, a position exemplified by African American disco diva Sylvester, an openly gay and flamboyant performer who had a succession of hit dance singles.[12] At worst, a black gay music artists' sexuality remained closeted, for fear that any acknowledgment of homosexuality would kill their career as an acceptable black entertainer. The life and career of black R&B artist Luther Vandross embodied such a career arc.[13] Because of these challenges, Prince's cross-dressing premier on *The Midnight Special* functioned as an insurgent politics of style that defined him as distinct from any R&B contemporaries of the period. In this regard, early in his career, Prince utilized androgyny, a sexual sensibility most associated with white cultural trends, social impulses, and emergent themes of the period, to establish and cultivate a white rock and roll aura.

While the 1960s was marked by multiple struggles around racial justice, women's equality, and the antiwar movement, the 1970s witnessed a sexual revolution that cropped up not just in the intimate spaces of American bedrooms but in the public sphere of white pop culture. Films such *Bob & Carol & Ted & Alice* (1969) acknowledged wife swapping as a thrilling alternative lifestyle, a form of sexual experimentation that gained mainstream traction to such an extent that the lifestyle even made inroads into America's national pastime when two professional baseball players swapped wives.[14] American pop culture also offered other options concerning one's sexual identity. For example, *The Rocky Horror Picture Show* (1975) became a cult film sensation starring a transvestite named Dr. Frank-N-Furter (Tim Curry) wearing fishnet stockings and a corset. In addition, American popular music celebrated sexual experimentation in the guise of fashionable queerness whereby white musicians, such as Lou Reed, Elton John, and, most dramatically, David Bowie, presented bisexuality as a point of intrigue and defiant entertainment.[15] Bowie deployed queer sexuality as a type of entertainment meets visual politics meets eroticism mash-up in the guise of a bisexual alien dressed in drag, on his critically acclaimed release *The Rise and Fall of Ziggy Stardust and the Spiders from Mars* (1972).

For better or worse, the theatrics of David Bowie's androgynous Ziggy Stardust transformed the rock musician into a character.[16] Moreover, Bowie's music characters also had racial implications, a point witnessed with the constructed nature of Bowie's post–glam rock release *Young Americans* (1975). No longer Ziggy Stardust, Bowie essentially played the part of a "white, British soul boy living out a fantasy of being black," with his earliest incarnation of his The Thin White Duke character.[17] Perhaps Prince borrowed most from Bowie for his sexy crooning cross-dresser bit and, like Bowie, Prince presented a series of transformations whereby a "character" corresponded to the type of music released for each successive album. Bowie, in his Thin White Duke guise, for a moment was about being black. For the first stage/televisual incarnation of Prince it was about not being pigeonholed as a black artist. The hyperconstructed nature of Prince's early style and stagecraft, post the *For You* release, privileged adrogyny and the homoerotic to cultivate a white rock and roll aura that is placed in sharp relief with the two versions of the "I Wanna Be Your Lover" video.

Through the power of special effects editing the "I Wanna Be Your Lover," video depicts Prince simultaneously appearing on screen playing bass guitar, drums, keyboards, and lead guitar and singing in front of a microphone stand. Clearly, the music video is meant to emphasize Prince's musical prowess by showing Prince playing all the instruments in the band. But the standout element of the video is Prince's performativity as a singer and how the video captures his flirtatious zeal. Prince sings directly into the camera, shimmies his shoulders to the rhythm of the music, and constantly flips his shoulder-length straightened hair to and fro. On the official "I Wanna Be Your Lover" video Prince exuded a "soft" androgynous sex appeal that signaled Prince's effeminate style. In this regard, Prince was like a black version of a young Leif Garrett, a 1970s long-haired, androgynous *Teen Beat* heartthrob.

Unlike the official "I Wanna Be Your Lover" release, the alternative music video release (which was never aired and rarely seen) features all the members of Prince's performance band: Gayle Chapman, Matt Fink, Bobby Z, André Cymone, and Dez Dickerson. Prince is bare chested, guitar slung over his shoulder, sporting baby blue satin dolphin shorts, silver lamé boots, and blue stockings worn as legwarmers. At various points Prince shares the microphone with Dez and André striking the familiar rock music poses of groups like the Rolling Stones and Led Zeppelin. Midway through the video Prince saunters over to Gayle as she comes from behind the keyboards. Prince pantomimes that he is caressing her face. In comparison to the musical camaraderie Prince demonstrates with his sidemen, the "sexual tension" between Chapman and Prince appears overly staged. Prince looks more at ease pining away about wanting to make love when singing close to his sidemen. Prince's early television performances and these two music videos make apparent that, across several different settings, Prince exudes and engages in a distinct homoerotic sensibility and interplay with erotic stage play.

On *The Midnight Special* performance of "I Wanna Be Your Lover," Prince only bumps and shimmies next to his male sidemen and showcases a "hard" drag presentation. For the official "I Wanna Be Your Lover," video Prince exudes a "soft" androgynous image. On American Bandstand he strikes the oxymoronic pose of a coquettish ingenue. The sum of Prince's visually dissonant images, at this juncture, appeared to demonstrate how his androgynous persona was not static. Moreover, Prince's transgressive sexual "character" also had racial ramifications. Prince's cross-dressing style and stagecraft functioned as a savvy attempt to distract and distance his music and himself from any R&B typecasting. Ultimately, Prince was going through all this stylistic rigmarole to cultivate a white rock and roll aura. But dabbling in cross-dressing was not just a white stylistic excursion that mimicked the glam rock androgyny of the 1970s and was most attuned to the imagination of white audiences. Black audiences were also intrigued and entertained by Rick James's androgynous aesthetic and the sexually transgressive impulses it symbolized. James was perhaps the only male black performer alongside Prince who was able to experiment in cross-dressing and compel a significant black fandom.

Prince's cross-dressing seemed to invite the audience to view Prince as gay, or at least bisexual. In comparison, Rick James was, and remained, ensconced in established notions of black masculinity even though "Slick" Rick, and the other male members of his Stone City Band, sported a brand of effeminate dandyism. They all wore long, braided hair extensions, often accented with beads and formfitting outfits. Rick James went even farther. He added glitter and bangs to his hairstyle along with tight spandex body suits, plunging necklines, and red thigh-high boots, a look he perfected on the album cover of the phenomenally funky and successful release *Street Songs* (1981). In addition, like Prince, James used heavy makeup, wore below-the-shoulder-length hair, and rocked high-heeled boots. Ironically, Prince toured on James's 1980 *Fire It Up* tour as an opening act, a gig that resulted in James claiming Prince had stolen his stage moves.[18] Nonetheless, the dramatic difference between their respective image and attempts at defining a popular representation of black masculinity for consumption was that Rick James was hyperheterosexual in his image construction. Prince was not.

In this context, James's appropriation of queer styling stands as qualitatively distinct from that of Prince, and symbolized broader intraracial tensions concerning the intersection of race, gender fluidity, and a black aesthetic. Through his appropriation of queer styling Rick James repetitively framed himself in relationship to heterosexual longing, a point underscored by incessant depictions of James in relationship to desiring females. For example, on the cover of Rick James's debut release *Come Get It!* (1978) is a picture of a long and lean black woman with almond-brown skin lying down in anticipation of Rick James. James floats above her, with his right arm fully extended and hand outstretched. The only thing ambiguous about the image is whether the sexually alluring pose and blissful body language of the model are in anticipation of James's touch or a result of it. *Come Get It!* was a multiplatinum smash LP driven by the soulful hit dance single "You and I" and the popular deep midtempo groove "Mary Jane," a poetic ode to the intoxicating powers of marijuana.

Subsequent James albums continued to incorporate gender-bending elements. On the *Fire It Up* (1979) album cover James wears high-heeled, thigh-high white boots with a white, rhinestone-accented, full-body spandex outfit topped off with a white Stetson hat. Despite James's queer styling his heterosexual appetite was overtly signified. The back cover of the *Fire It Up* album features a photo of a black female model straddling James's leg, as if she was riding a horse, while a white model is shown desperately trying to pull James away from her. In the end, James appeared more space cowboy than midnight cowboy. To his credit James also merged his hyperheteronormative representations with fantasy imagery that invoked the erotically charged fantasyscape of the comic magazine *Heavy Metal* (1977–2014) and animated film of the same name, *Heavy Metal* (1981). The magazine and the film presented all-white worlds full of violence and sexual mayhem populated by a mélange of scantily clad women with gratuitous cleavage and muscled men in loincloths wielding swords, shields, and ray guns.

James attempted to create a black version of white science fiction and fantasy erotica on his album covers. The cover of his *Bustin' Out of L Seven* (1978) album is a cartoon version of Rick James wielding his guitar like a weapon, flanked by three warrior maidens as he escapes through a shattered concrete wall. The *Throwin' Down* (1982) album cover shows James dressed like a black Conan the Barbarian in full sword and sorcery flair, a guitar serving semiotic double duty as an axe with the edge of it splattered with blood. The back cover of *Throwin' Down* has James pulling a warrior maiden up the staircase of a castle dungeon. Such erotic image construction marks James as a boundary-defying African American performer. Perhaps these erotic and daring displays of fantastic blackness contributed to James's image as the consummate "cocksman," his larger-than-life reputation as a person with a boundless sexual appetite, and cultivated an imagined (and lived) life-style of unbridled erotic heterosexual hedonism.

In stark contrast, Prince's album covers and back photos lacked James's visceral imagery of black heterosexual hedonism. Prince's album covers, at the least, intimated at an effeminate bisexual sensibility and, at most, a queer identity. Where Prince usurped James's erotic image was Prince's graphic and overt articulation of what type of sexual intercourse he desired and how he would perform particular sexual acts. Although songs about sex have always been a staple of black music Prince was shockingly literal. For example, before Prince a variety of blues songs of early bluesmen were primarily lewd testaments to the power of allusion. The titles of songs often functioned as subversive clues to the real sexual meaning of the content, a practice observed with Wynonie Harris's "Lollipop Mama" (1948) and "I Like My Baby's Pudding" (1950) or Muddy Waters's "I'm Your Hoochie Coochie Man" (1954). Barry White would continue this blues tradition with dance grooves that did double duty as de facto soundtracks for making love. Marvin Gaye would make more direct references concerning sex with songs like "Let's Get it On" (1971) and the track "You Sure Love to Ball" (1971), which provided simulated sounds of intercourse with soft ambient female cooing in the background.

Blues and soul men, however, were not the only ones getting off on wax. Donna Summer's appropriately titled song "Love to Love You Baby" (1975) took preorgasmic moaning to another level. The extended version of the down tempo disco track contained nearly seventeen minutes of deep groans and heavy breathing while R&B soul singer Millie Jackson's tart tongue increasingly left very little to the imagination when lovemaking was the topic. But Prince's third studio release, appropriately titled *Dirty Mind* (1980), was something altogether different. With *Dirty Mind*, Prince crafted a flawed, funky, and critically acclaimed masterpiece of sheer pornographic lewdness. Previous Prince songs from the *For You* and *Prince* releases presented sexually suggestive material like "Soft and Wet," "Sexy Dancer," and "Bambi," a lament over a former lover becoming a lesbian. In contrast, on *Dirty Mind* Prince infused the album with a substantial amount of sex magic, a sensibility signaled on the front and back album cover.

The front and back covers are shot in black and white and show Prince wearing a trench coat with a bandana tied around his neck. Beneath the trench coat he is bare-chested and sporting black bikini underwear that look more like women's panties than men's briefs. The back of the album shows Prince lying down in bed with his legs sheathed in thigh high black leggings, slightly bent and ajar. The picture leaves such a liberal amount of skin showing it is difficult to tell if he is still wearing his black bikini underwear at all. Scrawled on the white wall behind him in black spray paint are the title of the album and the name of the seven songs on the release. Both the front and back covers signal that Prince is, at best, a sexual outlaw and at worst, possibly a pervert.

Music critic Ken Tucker of *Rolling Stone* magazine deemed the stagecraft for the *Dirty Mind* album cover a breath of fresh air, an observation clearly articulated in his comment that the "cover photograph depicts our hero [Prince], smartly attired in a trench coat and black bikini briefs, staring soberly into the camera. The major tunes are paeans to bisexuality, incest, and cunnilingual technique. . . . At its best, *Dirty Mind* is positively filthy. Sex, with its lasting urges and temporary satisfactions, holds a fascination that drives the singer to extremes of ribald fantasy."[19] Prior to Prince, such sexually graphic content had a limited degree of popular success for black performers. Only the infamous Blowfly (Clarence Reid), a novelty act and cult underground character, with his pornographic parodies of popular songs, accrued any degree of success as a niche R&B performer given his sexually explicit "party" albums.

Dirty Mind was markedly different than anything Blowfly concocted. On the one hand, even though Prince upped the ante for sexual theatrics with songs promoting fellatio, such as "Head" (and would later release songs with titles such as "Pussy Control," "Scarlet Pussy," and "Orgasm"), Prince merged sexual explicitness with hit music making. On the other hand, successful hit-making R&B performers from the past or even Prince's early contemporaries, like Rick James, could not fully match his graphic sexuality. For example, James could only bring himself to allude to a woman's vagina as "that sweet funky stuff," on the track "Give It to Me." Prince's lyrics were more pornographic than provocative, and although Rick James was the self-professed freak, Prince periodically crossed over the threshold from freaky to filthy. A few lyrics from "Sister," a Prince song off the *Dirty Mind* release are enough to make the point: "My sister never made love to anyone else but me / She's the reason for my, uh, sexuality / Showed me where it's supposed to go / A blow job doesn't mean blow / Incest is everything it's said to be." Even decades later, "Sister" remains a bothersome track. The song invites the terribly sad and disturbing impression that any Prince song concerning sex is part of a deplorable personal experience.

If the song is not "true," then "Sister" is almost equally disturbing for what it suggests about a person that would manufacture a song about sibling sexual abuse as a lived experience when it was not and then choose to sing about it. Despite these dubious options for characterizing Prince's psychological state, simply stated, "Sister" is not about Prince. "Sister" is about punk and punk signposts and informs the post-punk sonic building blocks for what made Prince an innovative musical force. In this case, punk rock of the late 1970s and early 1980s properly decodes and correctly contextualizes "Sister" and reveals how the genre is fundamental to Prince's music and his future success. In terms of tone, punk rock of the late 1970s and early 1980s was a cynical condemnation of 1960s flower-power idealism and the subsequent saccharin soft rock ballads of the 1970s. The groundbreaking punk performer Richard Hell and the Voidoids' punk song "Love Comes in Spurts," flaunts, in the title alone, its contemptuous posture against and strident repudiation of "the dawning of the Age of Aquarius."

The punk movement also embraced taboo topics and often enacted a deliberate attempt at vulgarity, a posture that could also invite varying degrees of artifice and affect. In this regard, the lyrical content and message of punk music often flailed at being shocking as "a cultural-musical response to the music of the past and the social conditions of the present, presented as a fuck-you to the mainstream."[20] "Sister" unmistakably asserts an aesthetic attitude directly drawn from punk rock by conveying the idea that human sexuality is a pessimistic necessity and even a menacing specter. "Sister" signaled a punk sensibility and was in total opposition to Prince songs like "My Love Is Forever" and "I'm Yours" from the *For You* release and *Prince* material such as "When We're Dancing Close and Slow" and "I Feel for You."

In terms of instrumentation, "Sister" adopts the same sonic aesthetic as classic punk with its stripped down arrangement, a sparse lead guitar played in a fast and hard tempo against a rapid beat, and Prince keeping cadence with the jarring rhythm by shouting the lyrics in a clipped pace, a signature vocal aesthetic of punk rock akin to shouting more than singing. Furthermore, "Sister" clocks in at 1:31, a format also keeping with the punk standard of truncated song structure. Hence a radical reading of "Sister" firmly situates the track as rooted in the punk aesthetic of blunt and belligerent lyrics that disparaged prevailing sociopolitical mores and engaged sexual taboos as a form of political theater and cultural revolt.[21] At its best, "Sister" is Prince doing his interpretation of the punk thing on *Dirty Mind*, and in keeping with the punk rock thematic, demonstrated he has abandoned any utopian notions of love articulated on his previous full album releases. At its worst, "Sister" was a trite attempt at mimicking the disruptive energies that early punk rock articulated.

In the strictest sense of the punk aesthetic, because punk places a premium on authenticity, the punk pose Prince adopts for "Sister" is that of a poseur. Who could really believe that his sister pimped Prince out as a teenager any more than thinking a woman on the way to her wedding performed fellatio on Prince and married him instead? Unfortunately, Prince overcompensates or thoroughly misinterprets the punk ethos by suggesting, in at least one interview, that the songs of the *Dirty Mind* release had any credence in reality.[22] However, such musical stunts should not be uncritically condemned or simply dismissed. When artists make forays into other sonic settings it can yield aesthetic innovations and gratifying musical developments even if the broader political sensibility of the music is compromised. With "Sister," Prince put a premium on the shock factor of punk rock and appropriated the genre for its malleability to the sex-rock sensibility Prince suggested on *Prince* and shockingly crafted for *Dirty Mind*.

Arguably, *Dirty Mind* is the Rosetta stone for decoding Prince's subsequent body of work because it shows how Prince fuses an emergent musical genre, that seems almost antagonistic to his current or last musical style, with his own and repurposes it, a style and sensibility that quickly became a signature feature of Prince's music and image for years to come. With the *Dirty Mind* release Prince demonstrated, most impressively, his ability to fuse rock-guitar riffing (prominently previewed on "My Love Is Forever") with his keyboard-centered soul sound (overwhelmingly prevalent on "I Wanna Be Your Lover") and combine it with the emergent post-punk new wave sound of the early 1980s. Despite some punk proclivities, on the whole, *Dirty Mind* was a black new wave album indebted to punk rock. New wave music, a wide-ranging term, was more commercially viable with its hooks and dance rhythms than the edgy and underground-oriented punk rock. Nonetheless, new wave remained antiauthoritarian despite its punk-light disposition.

Admittedly, Prince was not the only black artist to incorporate the emergent punk and new wave sensibility into his style and sound. Fittingly, Rick James was an early innovator as well and adopted the "punk" nomenclature for his music. In the wake of disco's demise, James ditched his dance music tag for his self-coined term, "punk-funk." Arguably, this was more of a savvy maneuver meant to distance his brand of up-tempo dance music from disco, an increasingly despised music genre during the early 1980s. In contrast to James's made-up music terminology, Cameo, with the release of the album *Alligator Woman* (1982), offered an example of a bona fide black R&B band coopting the new wave sound for itself and on its own aesthetic terms. The title track, "Alligator Woman" was a remarkable testament of frenetic funkiness. "Alligator Woman" sounded like a funky version of the B-52s' "Rock Lobster," an emblematic version of the new wave sound of the period. By the late 1980s, Cameo cemented the interplay between new wave and R&B with discordant dance grooves like "Flirt," "She's Strange," "Attack Me with Your Love," "Single Life," "Candy," and "Back and Forth."

Artists such as Rick James and the group Cameo had cut their teeth on R&B, and new wave was more of a successful excursion from the tried and true R&B formula they had already mastered. In contrast, the new wave template grounded Prince's style and was paramount to his musical identity and sound. His synthesizer-based brand of new wave dance music took the emerging style and sound coming from London, England, and demonstrated how a white music genre and racial blackness were not necessarily antagonistic. Furthermore, the nexus between punk rock and new wave provided Prince not only a sonic template for future success but a clear visual and identifiable punk/new wave style that was relevant and of the moment, moving away from white rock tropes and almost totally detached from anything related to black R&B music and visual style. For as much as punk was a genre committed to a new sound, it was also about a particular type of visual presentation and performance.

Arguably, the deconstructed fashion of punk was as arresting as the music with the emergence of safety-pin-covered clothes, bondage gear, harsh androgyny, studded and ripped garments, as well as the Mohawk hairstyle. Most importantly, punk's sonic progeny, the new wave, would adopt an art-rock sensibility that also foregrounded a unique visual look. In the book

Are We Not New Wave: Modern Pop at the Turn of the 1980s, Theo Cateforis makes this astute observation concerning the visual template and specific color motif that often defined new wave groups:

> Dressed in slimmed, angular clothing—with a predominantly red, black and
> white color scheme—their attire mirrored the stripped-back demeanor of
> their music. . . . Whatever it's particular resonance, the red and black
> color scheme would come to define the new wave. . . . From the Romantics'
> matching red suits and Devo's red flower pot hats to Gary Numan's black and
> red belted jumpsuits and Chrissie Hynde's red leather jacket, seemingly
> everywhere one turned in 1980 new wave album covers were saturated in red
> and black fashion. It had become a de rigeur component of new wave style.[23]

Not only had Prince adopted a new wave sound for *Dirty Mind*, he also
dressed the part with a frazzled, and at times, spikey, short cut perm, red
bandanna tied around his neck, black leggings, and black jackets. Against
the emergent backdrop of new wave, Prince's look, style, and stagecraft were
no longer drawn from his recent past of cross-dressing glam rock, a trope
that undermined conventional notions of black R&B performance and marketing categorization. Instead, what was once a visual platform for Prince
to subvert traditional gendered notions of African American masculine and
feminine appearance became a statement that signified Prince's membership
in an emergent and predominantly white musical scene. As a consequence,
Prince's cross-dressing touches now signified the nascent new wave moment.

Prince would debut his new wave sensibility on national television by performing on *Saturday Night Live* (1975–present), a late night comedy sketch
show that showcased various guest musical artists. Although *Saturday Night
Live* (*SNL*) was positioned as an unconventional comedy show, it was rather
conservative regarding racial representation.[24] *SNL* appeared only obligated
to have one black comedian at a time, with Garret Morris in the 1970s and
Eddie Murphy in the early 1980s.[25] Given the blatant racial tokenism of the
cast of *SNL* the content of the show was clearly geared to address the tastes
and values of a white viewing audience. Interestingly, Prince, unlike a vast
majority of emerging black music artists of the period, was able to showcase
his new wave material on a television program geared toward a white audience. This booking signaled Prince, his music, his band and fandom existed
outside conventional R&B notions of Prince as a black performer.

On *Dirty Mind* Prince declared he promoted "revolutionary rock and roll," now he would have the chance to show and prove it with his performance of "Partyup," a song from the *Dirty Mind* release. On February 21, 1981, Prince appeared on *SNL* wearing black leggings and black bikini bottoms under a pale lavender trench coat and flanked by two trench-coated African American sidemen (wearing pants), with André Cymone on bass and Dez Dickerson playing electric guitar. The three remaining white members were buried behind the three upfront. Nonetheless, white keyboardist Matt Fink, the oddest and most incongruous member of Prince's backing band, helped to optically affirm Prince's new wave pedigree. Spastic nervousness, epitomized by white groups such as Devo and the Talking Heads, was a signature element of new wave performances.[26] Fittingly, Fink's herky-jerky performance on the cramped *SNL* stage visually epitomized the emergent new wave aesthetic with his frantic movements. Lastly, Prince undercut the funk R&B sonic elements of the album version of "Partyup" by performing the song at a considerably faster tempo and in a manic style for the *SNL* audience. At the conclusion of the song Prince and his band abruptly ran off the stage, knocking down the microphone stand as if someone had just yelled "Fire!" Without a doubt, the performance was scorching hot.

The *SNL* musical showcase also marks how Prince aligned himself with the proven antiauthoritarian politics of punk and the emergent new wave style of the period. He clearly sang the words "fucking war" during his "Partyup" performance, proving he was no longer the awkward mumbling music prodigy lip-syncing on *American Bandstand*. Now, he was a bona fide trench-coated sexual outlaw. Regrettably, the show is mostly discussed for marking the nadir of the *SNL* series before a massive firing and dramatic recasting rather than the energetic immediacy of Prince's performance in front of a live *SNL* audience.[27] Fortunately, the promotional music videos for "Dirty Mind" and "Uptown" replicated the live-audience immediacy that Prince delivered on *SNL*.

The "Dirty Mind" and "Uptown" videos looked like real concert footage from Prince's *Dirty Mind* Tour. Interestingly, the videos contained numerous shots of a racially mixed but predominantly white audience dancing and enjoying the show. The racially mixed concert audience signaled Prince was a crossover artist adored by whites even more than blacks and provided visual proof that Prince's music represented the sonic embodiment of America as a racial melting pot. In reality, Prince and his band were lip-synching live performances on an indoor stage in front of an artificial audience. As a result, both music videos were examples of stylized faux-concert footage. Nevertheless, the videos offered a vision of Prince that worked to undermine strident racial notions that a black music artist could not garner white music fans. But the question remained. Would a real audience of white music fans respond to Prince in the same enthusiastic manner depicted in his music videos? Prince soon discovered the answer to this question as an opening act for the Rolling Stones, one of the most legendary white rock bands in the music industry.

In the early 1980s, with the release of their eighteenth studio album *Tattoo You* (1981) and supporting tour, the Rolling Stones were reaching their commercial peak in America, even though the Stones were deep into the proverbial "second-act" of their career. The single from *Tattoo You* was the appropriately titled "Start Me Up," and reached #2 on the American *Billboard* music chart. Most importantly, given Mick Jagger's own androgynous showmanship and blues sensibility, Prince's gender-bending rhythm and rock appeared a good match as the opening act for their tour. On October 9 and 11, 1981, fresh off the critical success of *Dirty Mind* but not a household-name performer, Prince and his band took the stage and faced a sea of nearly 100,000 people staring back at them.[28] Prince tried to account for the rock sensibility of the audience by cherry-picking his set list with the rock-oriented track "Bambi" and the rockabilly-inflected "Jack U Off," a tune that relied more on guitar riffs than synthesizer vamps. Despite auspicious similarities between Jagger and Prince the latter was not well received at the Los Angeles Coliseum. Ultimately, no amount of guitar thrashing was enough to negate the ill-suited titles and could not win over the overwhelmingly white rock audience.

Prince and his backing band members (Mark Brown had replaced André Cymone on bass guitar) were pelted with objects and summarily booed off the stage.[29] As a result, Prince made a hurried exit all the way to Minneapolis. Dez Dickerson, however, convinced him to come back to Los Angeles and play the next scheduled gig; it was déjà vu all over again. Prince was summarily booed off the stage. Most likely, the Rolling Stones' audience were album-oriented rock fans on their way to becoming classic rock enthusiasts, a sleazy synthesizer-centered track, like "Uptown," did not stand a chance at abating the racial slurs used to berate Prince or halting the bottle and food throwing the band endured. In any event, the racial optics of three black men playing guitar in a massive open stadium, filled with antagonistic white rockers, was a stark contrast to the controlled indoor environment of the studio stage where Prince made his *Dirty Mind* music videos in front of an adoring predominantly white audience.

Prince yearned for "Uptown," a place where blacks, whites, and Puerto Ricans (the symbolic proxy for all other racial minorities) are free to be themselves and interact with one another musically or in other intimate ways. The audience's reaction to Prince as a black performer opening for the Rolling Stones demonstrated that not only was "Uptown" ephemeral but Prince was far from achieving colorblind crossover success. In the end, *Dirty Mind* primarily impressed a predominantly white rock music press to take notice of Prince, not a primarily white rock audience to do the same. On Prince's next album, *Controversy* (1981), he abandoned pining for the type of racial utopia suggested on "Uptown." In contrast, the title track, "Controversy," resembled a lament.

Perhaps the disappointing, if not traumatic, dismissal of his music and image at the Rolling Stones' concert, by a predominantly white audience, fueled the pointed questions Prince rhetorically asked on the "Controversy" track when he sang, "Am I black or white? / Am I straight or gay?— Controversy." Later, on the same track Prince states, "I wish there was no black or white / I wish there were no rules." With *Dirty Mind* Prince signaled an obsession with sex that was thrillingly treacherous, vulgar, and periodically perverse. The *Controversy* release signaled that sex was not only a point of intense interest, possible salvation, but also an expression of racial liberation. Prince's desire for a world devoid of racial distinction is clearly articulated in the lyrics of "Sexuality," a single from the *Controversy* release. Prince sings on "Sexuality": "I'm talking about a revolution, we gotta organize / We don't need no segregation, we don't need no race / New age revelation, I think we got a case / I'm okay as long as you are here with me / Sexuality is all we ever need." Without a doubt, sex magic is pitched as the panacea to all the problems present in the modern world. "Sexuality" signposted that Prince was not only ready to reject any racial labels that would impinge on his music and his image but that both his music and image transcended categorization.

As far as Prince's image for the *Controversy* release, Prince decided to accentuate his increasingly new wave sensibility. On the album cover Prince sported a starched white shirt buttoned up to his neck under a black vest accented with a bolero-like necktie. A lavender trench coat with a button pinned to the lapel of his coat that stated "Rude Boy" finished the look.

Prince still gazed into the camera with his signature blank stare. Ultimately, the *Controversy* album cover proclaimed Prince's newfound mod status, a revivalist style fueled by early 1980s punk and the new wave style that originally arose as an insurgent fashion in the United Kingdom during the 1960s.[30] In addition, the two promotional videos for the *Controversy* release showcased Prince's new personal style even though the "Controversy" and "Sexuality" videos repeated the visual formula from previous music videos. Both videos showed Prince and his backup band performing in a soundstage saturated in floodlights. The only compelling source of optic attention for the "Controversy" video was a brightly oversized stained glass window erected in the background of the soundstage, a look that suggested the stage was also a religious cathedral.

The stagecraft for the "Sexuality" video was even less optically interesting. The video deployed a green laser light show in a fog-filled soundstage. Prince tries to add some sexual sizzle by slowly removing his shirt toward the conclusion. Neither the laser effects nor Prince's striptease lent any air of erotic ambiance to the video; rather it made the entire performance appear corny. Nevertheless, the raw and polymorphous sexuality that Prince proclaimed on *Dirty Mind* was still present on *Controversy*, just increasingly stylized and marketed smarter. For instance, there was a promotional color pinup poster of Prince inside the *Controversy* album. Prince is shown standing in the shower wearing only black bikini underwear, with water cascading over him. Prince stares straight ahead, inviting the observer to "do me baby like you never done before."

In terms of the music, *Controversy* was a mixed bag. The *Controversy* material was more mature and less literal than the sex-infused *Dirty Mind*, a release that left little to the imagination. At its best, many of the synth-pop keyboard hooks, drum-machine beats, and rhythm guitar riffs sounded like precursors to techno music. At its worst, *Controversy* sounded sparse, mechanical, and straining to add a political punch to the erotic veneer Prince had established up to that point. The singles "Controversy" and "Let's Work" could only scale the R&B charts at #3 and #9, respectively. In Prince's recent past, *For You* and, to a lesser extent, *Prince* were albums in search of a clear point of departure and a signature frame of reference. *Dirty Mind* was the experiment that succeeded in gaining white attention, and *Controversy* was the PG-13 follow-up to discover if the X-rated *Dirty Mind* was a fluke. More importantly, *Dirty Mind* and *Controversy* allowed Prince to experiment and refine his image. However, before Prince could lay claim to a broader audience and white crossover success he would have to make a few more image transformations.

Sex was all Prince would ever need (at least for quite a while) to provide a distinct thematic to his burgeoning body of work. Undeniably, Prince was sticking with exploring the fetishistic outskirts of human sexuality, and the topic would serve as the core of Prince's lyrical content in the immediate future. Masturbation, sadomasochism, fantasy intercourse, one-night stands in multiple positions, odes to various body parts, orgasms, and fucking until dawn are the short list of sex-related material Prince would cover. Nevertheless, Prince was still unable to use hypersexuality as a foil to fully negate the racial constricts of the period. Even though Prince had performed on national television shows, such as *American Bandstand*, *The Midnight Special*, and *Saturday Night Live*, mainstream success remained marginal. White critics took notice of him, but black audiences were the ones listening and, most importantly, purchasing his music.

In the wake of *Dirty Mind* and *Controversy* Prince was perilously close to being typecast as a weirdo and merely attaining a cult following interested in the shock value of his sexually charged material. With his next release, the sonic opus *1999* (1982), Prince would benefit from the evolving centrality of music videos for marketing and mainstream exposure. With music videos, visual charisma was just as important as shocking lyrics and exceptional musical talent. To that end, the music video was the preeminent medium for Prince throughout the 1980s, and with *1999* Prince consolidated image, sound, and attitude into the figure of a purple-clad pied piper of synth-pop sexual revelry dedicated to leading his music followers ecstatically dancing into judgment day.

In this regard, Prince became the embodiment of a modern-day Dionysus. On the surface, such image construction appeared accurate. At a deeper level, Prince more accurately represented a two-faced Janus peering in opposite directions. One face was racially ambiguous and gazing toward a mainstream horizon of MTV white crossover success. The other face a black doppelganger, rooted in the style, taste, and sensibility of black culture, gazed toward black America and the R&B charts.

2

On the Black Hand Side

> *Prince's success in overcoming musical and racial boundaries has not just directly (through his many protégés) and indirectly (through those he influenced) affected 1980's popular music. He has also done much to lessen the de facto segregation of black artists that had arisen in the early 80's on radio and in the televising of music videos.*
> —John Rockwell, Music Critic

> *"Jamie Starr's a thief! / It's time to fix your clock!"*
> —Prince, "D.M.S.R."

In *Blues People: Negro Music in White America* (1963), Amiri Baraka detailed how black music, like black people, either synthesized or remained estranged from white cultural tastes. What Baraka paid less attention to, when it came to black music, was the reverse process. In pre-1950s America, African Americans were primarily associated with driving the popularity of what was called "race music "and "race records," the racial nomenclature of the time for black music. By the 1960s there was an increasing degree of white popularity and profitability associated with black music; young American white consumers had become increasingly enthusiastic about black music, having enjoyed the doo-wop and early rhythm and blues styles popularized in the 1950s. Eventually, white artists and their record labels tried to usurp the cresting popularity of black artists and appropriate the sound and style of their music by having white musicians cover songs originally recorded and performed by black artists. For example, Pat Boone covered Fats Domino's "Ain't That a Shame" (1955) and Little Richard's "Tutti Frutti" (1955). Moreover, Boone epitomized the most notorious example of a mediocre white performer shooting to the top of the mainstream music charts by covering the notable songs of black artists.[1] The results were often a toned-down and diluted white version of the original black song. Nonetheless, the cultural implication of white artists "covering" black creative material was clear. White culture and tastes were being shaped by black folk, and whites were aping the sounds and rhythms of black America.

By the 1960s, with the emergence of the Motown record label (a black record company), the aesthetic pilfering that white artists committed against black music was increasingly diminished. Berry Gordy, the founder of Motown Records, perfected a black pop sound that was nearly impossible to duplicate by white imitators, and it was also preferred by white consumers.[2] The "Motown Sound" was an impressive bulwark against the aesthetic pilfering and creative inroads white artists were making with early rhythm and blues music and exemplified a new form of black crossover success that both black and white music fans adored. Nonetheless, the mainstream crossover pop appeal of the Motown Sound would also draw criticism as a formula that appeared to prod black musicians to abandon their core black audience to privileged crossover success with whites.[3] A few years after Motown's brief reign as America's soundtrack throughout the 1960s, another emergent popular music genre, called disco, reanimated similar racial debates around black authenticity and white crossover impulses during the mid-1970s.

In the early 1970s disco music began as black dance music played in black gay underground clubs that soon ceded to racially integrated dance floors, whereby blacks, Latinos, and whites shuffled and twirled together at the same time as white singers, that sounded black, sung on various disco tracks.[4] By 1979, however, there was a backlash against disco. Ostensibly, under the rhetorical edict that "disco sucks," the mechanical and commercial hedonism of disco was attacked, but beneath the shrill criticisms about how vapid the music had become lurked another motivation. The anti-disco campaign also reflected growing hostility and frustration with America's changing sexual mores and increasingly porous racial boundaries represented by disco.[5] The response was a retrenchment of racial segregation in the American music industry whereby album-oriented rock and arena stadium concert shows supplanted the dance singles and discotheque venues that were the cornerstones of disco music as a genre and club community, a sensibility represented in the film *Saturday Night Fever* (1977) and its soundtrack. Against this shifting undercurrent of hostility toward transgressive sexual politics and racial integration in society, on the dance floor, and on wax, Prince not only made his musical debut, he also navigated and negotiated when, and how, he could be black. In this case, Prince chose to be his blackest under the pseudonym of Jamie Starr and under the guise of a band named The Time.

The Time fronted a light-skinned African American lead singer named Morris Day. The other band members were Terry Lewis (bass player), Jimmy Jam (keyboards), Jellybean Johnson (drums), Monte Moir (keyboards), and Jesse Johnson (guitar). On the cover of their self-titled debut album, *The Time* (1981), the six-member group is pictured standing outside of some nondescript building wearing jacket blazers and shirts accented with skinny-ties, a new wave fashion staple of the 1980s. On the back cover the band stood facing the wall with their hands up as if they were waiting for the police to frisk them for contraband. The album consisted of a meager six songs and the overall running time for the entire album was forty-two minutes (it was still lengthier that the thirty-two-minute *Dirty Mind*). But the LP had two hit songs; "Get It Up" and "Cool," two extended jams of exquisite synth-funk orchestration.

"Get It Up" clocks in at just over nine minutes, a format that rejected radio-friendly packaging. It provided a funky blend of down-tempo, synth-electro, bass-heavy grooves punctuated by sleazy guitar riffs. "Get It Up" never feels labored or monotonous, and the driving instrumental keyboard and guitar solos interspersed toward the second half on the track keep the song stimulating and engaging to the ear. Similarly, "Cool" is an extended dance track that clocks in at just over ten minutes. This song, more than any other, consolidates the persona of Morris Day as a playful ladies man. "Cool" is also a classic example of the toast, a black folk tradition of a signifying, fanciful, and boastful tale told with a rhyming style of wordplay, often centered around a black male protagonist.[6] On the song, Day brags about his ultra-rich playboy lifestyle full of penthouses on both coasts, exotic cars, diamonds on his fingers and toes, a Learjet, fine women, and money by the ton. Later the song breaks into another staple of the black aesthetic, a call and response section between Day and the band about not being hot because they are—cool.

Last, but not least, is the more obscure track, "The Stick," a sophisticated down-tempo jam that suffered from a simple metaphor. The car's stick shift alluded to Day's erect penis and possibly male masturbation. Day sings "You just come too quick / I'd rather work my stick / Get a little satisfaction / work the stick in my ride." The lyrics were underdeveloped but the musicianship was complex. The track features a driving bass line loaded with thumping and popping licks reminiscent of when Larry Graham played electric bass guitar with Sly and the Family Stone. The stripped-down arrangement has a sleazy, rhythmic, synthesizer hook coupled with intricate keyboard solos and sparse vocals. In addition, the piano solo on "The Stick" is a pure joy of blues-inspired funk punctuated with syncopated soul claps. In stark contrast, the other three tracks were strictly filler that just took up space. "Girl," and "Oh, Baby" were two bubblegum slow jams and "After Hi School" was a trite, midtempo track that sounded like a rejected demo for a John Hughes teenage comedy film. Nevertheless, and on the whole, the album was a success and reached #7 on the R&B charts on the strength of "Get It Up" and "Cool."

Roughly four months after the release of the album, The Time made their television premiere on *Soul Train* (1971–2008) in November 1981. *Soul Train* was, without a doubt, a dance show geared toward black audiences and the established venue for launching new black music acts considered hot properties.[7] The group gave an inspired lip-sync karaoke performance of "Get It Up," and after their performance Don Cornelius, the inimitable host of *Soul Train*, interviewed the group. Cornelius complimented Monte Moir on his impressive keyboard musicianship and commented on the interesting "look" of the band. Cornelius then proceeded to mention that The Time originated from Minneapolis and asked Morris Day if he was responsible for the idea of the band. Day emphatically affirmed The Time was solely the product of his vision.

In retrospect, Cornelius's comments are peculiar given that he draws attention to the group's Minneapolis origin and never mentions Prince, Minneapolis's most famous musician. Moreover, The Time and Prince shared the same production personnel, an engineer named Jamie Starr. Below the back cover photograph of *The Time* album, and written in ordinary font, is a credit asserting that Morris Day and Jamie Starr are the musical masterminds of the group. Interestingly, Jamie Starr is credited as the engineer on Prince's *Dirty Mind* album. Given their same regional origin and shared musical engineer, it appeared quite odd to believe The Time and Prince were strangers to one another and only related by regional happenstance. All the same, circa 1981, The Time and Prince seemed like separate entities until you gave *The Time* album a deep second listen. Even though Prince was nowhere credited on The Time's debut album, the sonic similarities between The Time and Prince were too close to believe it was coincidental.

Never mind the visual resemblance of Morris Day to Prince, with their high-yellow complexions and similar chemically relaxed hairstyles. The music was the sonic tipoff. The instrumentation and musicianship on *The Time* album shared several of the same aural earmarks as most of the R&B-styled Prince jams of that period. For example, all the elements that made "I Wanna Be Your Lover" a hot track were increased and perfected on "Get It Up." The latter track also contained a heavy synthesizer, a catchy arrangement, and, most important, a long duration of instrumental vamping over a propulsive groove. Second, the version of "Get It Up," sung by the personnel on the *Soul Train* television stage never jives with the album version of "Get It Up" or the music video for "Cool." Most strikingly, "Get It Up" has two different male voices singing lead and background vocals at various points on the track, a feat that is not repeated with The Time's *Soul Train* performance. Why? Because the other voice is Prince, and the music is too.[8]

Prince performed and recorded the music along with singing all the vocals on *The Time* tracks. By the time Morris Day shows up in the studio, Prince directs Morris to mimic his vocal intonations, a fact revealed in the book *Prince: Inside the Music and the Masks*: "Prince played the new band [The Time] the completed music. Each number had his [Prince] voice singing the lyric. When Morris came over, Prince coached Morris on how to match every phrase and intonation. . . . Coyly, instead of removing his voice entirely, Prince left it on, so people could occasionally hear it right alongside Day."[9] Basically, under the pseudonym of Jamie Starr and under the guise of a band, Prince created a black cover version of himself. The Time was Prince and Prince was The Time. With its stripped-down arrangement the standout tracks from *The Time* release are evocative of a more soulful version of

Prince's *Dirty Mind* album, with Prince playing his most blatant musical incarnation of a "soul man" playing "black" music. In this deep cover, Prince, the performer, was obscured, but the fact remained that Prince, the musician, was funky, real funky.

At first, Prince's elaborate ruse was a great setup and the catalyst for a productive symbiotic relationship. Prince could reap the monetary reward from his musical incarnation, release a variety of R&B-leaning music without impinging on his pop music persona as a solo artist, and have The Time as an opening act for future tours. On Prince's *Controversy* tour the extended nature of the tracks on *The Time* album nicely fit the requirements of an opening act. The Time had just enough material to warm the crowd up but not too much to upstage the main act (in the beginning). Certainly, Prince's music was the calling card of The Time, but it was the look and charismatic attitude of Morris Day, and to a lesser extent the entire band, that made The Time a captivating unit.

Because the music Prince created in the studio required a superior set of music chops to pull off his arrangements on tour, the musicians he hired required an impressive degree of talent. In view of that, The Time not only played the music, they also honed a range of dance routines while playing their instruments, a stylized and streamlined version of the synchronized dance steps of old Motown groups like the Temptations.[10] The showmanship elements of this successful formula proved foremost in making the relationship between The Time and Prince problematic. By the time the group released its second album, *What Time Is It?*, the band was a well-synchronized group of musician-performers that had ironed out their performance kinks during the *Controversy Tour*. Ultimately, the *Controversy Tour* (1981–1982) served as an incubator for the formation of Morris Day as a charismatic lead singer and stage persona and perfected the visual showmanship of The Time to the point where they could upstage Prince. As The Time gained mounting popularity with their live shows and R&B-centered sound, what started as a simple plan to provide another outlet for Prince's material became an intense rivalry between Prince and The Time.[11]

Unlike the first release, Day was no longer an ultra-hip singer in an ultra-hip band. Instead, on the group's second release, *What Time Is It?*, Day was the literal face of the group. Morris Day is pictured alone on the cover, sporting a big bouffant-styled perm, pursed lips, a heavy application of eyeliner that makes his eyes bug out, and a "limp wrist" pose to visually call attention to his wristwatch, a modern-day imitation "Little" Richard. *What Time*

Is It? indicated Day's increasing prominence, a point signaled on the album cover and by having the other Time band members relegated to the back cover, along with a change in Day's character. On the band's self-titled debut, Day exhibited the style of a droll-talking dandy. On the sophomore release, however, Day was increasingly sophomoric in his outlook, observations, and language. While the music was still funky, silly talk became the centerpiece of the album's content. On tracks such as "The Walk," a track similar in tone to "Cool," Day engaged in monologues about the type of shoes he likes, the women he wants, and the pants he wears. At the time, Morris's "mack" seemed cool, but in retrospect his lines were corny conceits, and on one occasion they sounded just plain creepy. How else can you characterize a man that says things such as, "Who me? / I wear baggies / zip, snap, and drop / Easy access baby / Yes, before you get a chance to holler stop." Simply stated the stanza is an ode to date rape. Despite these weaknesses, *What Time Is It?* climbed to #2 on the R&B charts on the strength of two tracks, "The Walk" and "777-9311."

Both tracks are extended jams. "The Walk," with its lengthy vocal interludes dubbed over the music, is nearly ten minutes long, and "777-9311," clocks in just under eight minutes, a high-hat, drumming-infused, rhythmic jam that comes surprisingly close to affecting the pulsating groove of Clyde Stubblefield's legendary break-beat from "The Funky Drummer" (1970). The only sonic element more compelling than the drum programming from "777-9311," is the cascading waves of reverb generated by a virtuoso guitar solo. Arguably, the sexy synth-keyboard vamping ballad "Gigolos Get Lonely Too" solidified the release as a bona fide R&B hit album. Interestingly, no videos were made of any tracks. Maybe the lack of promotional music videos for The Time's sophomore release portended Prince's shrewd assessment that the group stood a chance at growing more popular than he was. Nonetheless, the elaborate ruse did prove Prince could deliver sonically when it came to creating black popular music. Prince's next side-project, Vanity 6, hewed closer to Prince's own new wave sensibility and embrace of the seemingly all-white music genre, even though Day boasted, "We don't like new wave," on the Prince penned and performed "The Walk."

The female group Vanity 6 burst onto the music scene in 1982 with their self-titled release *Vanity 6*. The core of the all-female trio was Denise Matthews (aka Vanity), an aspiring actress from Canada. Matthews inhabited the role of a delicate dominatrix. Susan Moonsie and Brenda Bennett were the two other members of the group. Moonsie embodied the problematic fantasy of a "Lolita," a sexually mature yet underage teenage girl, by dressing in white lingerie and always carrying a stuffed teddy bear. Rounding out the group was Brenda Bennett, a cigarette-smoking "butch" tough girl with an attitude.[12] Of this trio, Matthews was not only the lead singer of the group, she was Prince's female doppelgänger. Like Prince, Denise's career was a collection of transgressive articulations of human sexuality. Prior to her stint as Vanity she starred in *Tanya's Island* (1980), a soft-core, semipornographic B-movie that dabbled in bestiality. In the film, Matthews played a model stranded on an island inhabited by a gorilla that she is attracted to, and vice versa. Consequently, it was a profound improvement for Matthews to take on the character of an alluring lead singer in a real music group, even though the job had her crooning lyrics about wanting "seven inches or more" and insisting "its time to jam / nasty girls, dance, dance, dance." In this sense, Vanity herself and Vanity 6 as a group were as much or more about image than about content.

Vanity 6 performed in skimpy lingerie outfits paired with pumps, and a look that invited the male gaze to linger on their figures. In fact, in the video for "Nasty Girl" the trio is suggestive of a soft-core pornographic version of Motown's Supremes. All three women traipse into a dressing room lobby area in their civilian clothes, then midway through the song, go off-camera and return in lingerie to perform an out-of-sync dance routine to finish the video. Unfortunately, the *Vanity 6* release was judged more as a novelty act rather than a significant or even memorable album, a point apparently affirmed, until recently, by a decades-long out-of-print-status for the album. Without a doubt, the cobbled together trio was made of mediocre singers, at best, and they certainly were not musicians. Given the *Vanity 6* album barely generated thirty-one minutes of music across eight tracks, perhaps people did purchase the album and various singles merely to look at the front and back covers. In retrospect, however, *Vanity 6* is an important release because of the music, and the music was Prince. Of course Prince tried to displace his involvement with Vanity 6 (and The Time) by assigning creative credit to Jamie Starr as the groups' music producer or having his groups assert their lead role in creating the group. For example, on *Soul Train*, after Vanity 6's debut television performance, Don Cornelius interviewed the trio of women, and they claimed that they had written and produced all of the music on their release. This claim was as flimsy as the lingerie Vanity 6 wore on stage and gyrated in for the "Nasty Girl" music video. Prince was the mastermind of the project and responsible for virtually all the music.

You could hear Prince's signature funky keyboard arrangements and gui-tar riffs on too many tracks. The standout track was "Nasty Girl," a song that achieved commercial success as a breakout number one dance single and charted in the top ten on the R&B singles list. The song boasted an exotic synth hook and sultry bass line topped off with a snake charmer riff that hypnotized many a listener. Besides, anyone that listened to the track, "If a Girl Answers (Don't Hang Up)," would hear Prince on the song; he played the role of a trash-talking woman on the other end of a phone conversation with Vanity and Brenda. Despite the disavowals of Prince's involvement, on the *Vanity 6* release, he scored another R&B success with "Nasty Girl." On the whole, however, *Vanity 6* was more sonically aligned with the Go-Go's, a groundbreaking all-white female new wave band.

The Go-Go's made their debut with the killer album *Beauty and the Beat* (1981). With hindsight speculation fully in reverse, Vanity 6's "He's So Dull" sounds like a blatant bid at reproducing the Go-Go's "Our Lips Are Sealed," a retro-rock-inspired girl group pop song. Admittedly, "He's So Dull" proved too tedious a track to garner hit status like the Go-Go's "Our Lips Are Sealed," but the Vanity 6 song did break through into the mainstream, sort of. "He's So Dull" was featured in the film *National Lampoon's Vacation* (1983) and on the soundtrack for the hit film. In the end, Prince's sonic dis-avowals began to unravel for all to see when he snagged a coveted cover shot and story for the preeminent monthly music periodical *Rolling Stone* magazine. The *Rolling Stone* magazine banner headline for the cover read, "Prince's Hot Rock: The Secret Life of America's Sexiest One-Man Band."[13] The picture on the front of the magazine had Vanity draped behind Prince with her hand partially tucked inside the waistband of his pants; a sexually evocative stance that signaled their musical relationship was just as intimate as their pose. The phrase "one-man band" was also used in the article, a catchphrase that intimated Prince was making all the music on his releases but also suggested he was making music for other groups as well. After the *Rolling Stone* cover, it was an open secret that Prince was the sonic force behind The Time and Vanity 6, and no sonic sleuthing was needed to uncover the truth about Prince's involvement in these "black" side projects.

In retrospect, only George Clinton was a black recording artist confident enough to openly release various albums under two different groups. As Funkadelic, Clinton fronted an acid rock and funk group, and as Parlia-ment, he released the more R&B funk-friendly chart-scoring material. Clinton used these two groups to work through various sonic configurations and experiment with the potency of his funk stew, an amalgamation of elaborate instrumentality, rhythmic grooves, science fiction, Afrofuturism, heavy horns, and extended jamming. Similarly, Prince, under the Jamie Starr pseudonym, honed his musical chops and experimented with conventional notions of black music with The Time and Vanity 6. The only exception is that Clinton was an active and visible participant in both of his groups. At the time, critics like Nelson George, a prodigious and often pugnacious black music journalist, saw Prince's career as a purposeful capitulation and blatant expression of racial assimilation and, at worst, a professional posture that appeared antiblack.[14] But viewing Prince's career under the Jamie Starr pseudonym complicates such critiques. Admittedly, of the two side projects The Time has held up the best as a legitimate group and source of superior R&B musicianship. But a closer inspection of the Vanity 6 release is quite telling as a forerunner to Prince's next studio release, the genre-defying approach and sound of *1999* (1982).

Prince released *1999* a mere two months after the *Vanity 6* release. *1999* was filled with exotic R&B textures complemented with an eclectic array of new wave music fused with rock and roll accents. On the surface, the sonic similarities between the two albums appeared unrelated, but for a keen and ardent listener the likenesses were glaringly apparent. The droll vocals and extended length of "Automatic" (*1999*), were similar to the tone and sonic style of "Drive Me Wild" (*Vanity 6*). The drum programming on "All the Critics Love U in New York" was evocative of the drumming sequence of "Make Up," and "Delirious" was a new wave rockabilly version of *Vanity 6*'s "He's So Dull." *Vanity 6* was an undercooked and incomplete sonic buffet of Prince's emergent sound, whereas *1999* was a full-course, perfectly plated banquet.

On the one hand, tracks like "Let's Pretend We're Married," "Little Red Corvette," and "Delirious," melded new wave with a pop-rock sensibility. On the other hand, songs such as "Lady Cab Driver," an ode to hard humping, with its driving bass line, and "D.M.S.R.," with its minimalist dance groove, proved experimental funk masterpieces. "International Lover," a soulful power ballad, closed out the album on a more traditional R&B note. All the aforementioned tracks were exemplars of the emergent, original, and multidimensional hybrid sound Prince was crafting. On *1999* Prince was literally making music that defied categorization, going so far as to forsake a horn section, a sonic staple of black dance music. Even the genre-defying Sly and the Family Stone included wind and brass instrumentation in its tangy musical gumbo mix of rock, funk, gospel, and soul textures. By Prince excluding horns early in his music career he created a "new" style of black music, a sound that cracked the top ten on the *Billboard* 200 chart at #9, while the "1999" video broke through MTV's strident Jim Crow programming.

With the debut of MTV in 1981, and given how the cable television channel displaced the centrality of radio airplay for commercial success, visual charisma was just as important as musical talent.[15] Renowned music scholar Simon Frith best speaks to the prominent place of television for the commerce of music. For Frith, "TV's role in the record sales process means that looking good on television has always been essential for success. . . . The fact is that for the vast majority of people—particularly the vast majority of youth (and including the minority who themselves become performers)—rock stars are first seen on television, and what a rock star is meant to be is therefore to an extent defined by television."[16] With music videos, the image "toured" before, and frequently more often than, the actual band or artist and frequently sparked a manic demand that drove record sales. As a result, MTV airplay emerged as the lynchpin to generating successful and sustained music careers. Although MTV was a radical disruption of the music industry's marketing model, black artists remained all but nonexistent on MTV given that MTV programming was no different than radio's programming.[17] In the 1970s, the shift toward album-oriented rock (AOR) programming on various FM stations across the nation severely excluded black artists on mainstream radio stations. When MTV emerged, the racial marginalization present on radio was compounded by MTV because the cable channel courted the same white demographic audience.

Ironically, the commitment to AOR rock videos created an opening for black performers to squeeze onto MTV because MTV lacked American rock music videos to fulfill the programming commitment to exclusively play rock music. Music scholar Theo Cateforis sheds light on MTV's predicament and the opening it created for black artists:

> In its initial planning stages, MTV director Robert Pittman and the head of talent and acquisitions, Carolyn Baker, had sought to market the new video network as if it were a traditional "AOR channel," one whose music videos would cater to an already well-established white rock audience. Pittman found, however, that not only were many U.S. record labels skeptical of the new format's potential and thus uncooperative with the fledging network, but also that the majority of American rock artists who had relied on the

surefire publicity of radio were not even prepared with promotional clips that MTV could air. The British new pop bands, on the other hand, had been experimenting with the emergent medium for some time and arrived with stylish videos in hand. They found themselves in a serendipitous position, and MTV was eager to welcome them into its rotation.[18]

British pop bands, unlike their American counterparts, regularly incorporated African American music elements ranging from soul to roots reggae rhythms. Consequently, black British artists cropped up on MTV and were the first ones to chip away at the informal system of music apartheid the station had erected. As a result, British alternative music and artists not only gained the opportunity for mainstream exposure, their incursion opened a space for exotic blackness to earn a limited space for representation on MTV, a development that later proved serendipitous for Prince.

At first, MTV filled there twenty-four-hour video programming demands with a rash of British new wave and European electronic pop groups like Human League, ABC, Duran Duran, Depeche Mode, Thomas Dolby, Soft Cell, Billy Idol, and Culture Club, and the Australian groups INXS and Men at Work. In particular, music videos such as Human League's "Don't You Want Me" (1981), Culture Club's "Do You Really Want to Hurt Me" (1982), Thomas Dolby's "She Blinded Me with Science (1982)," and The Eurythmics' "Sweet Dreams Are Made of This" (1983) provided audiences with appealing artists and captivating visuals. Most importantly, as a direct by-product of this programming trend the more dance-oriented music videos challenged and displaced the relatively staid nature of most AOR music and performers. Consequently, hyperstylized videos came to dominate the MTV rotation.

Take for example, the video for Eddie Grant's electronic reggae platinum pop single "Electric Avenue" (1982). The film noir–like video was a brooding visual masterpiece that constantly cropped up on MTV. The signature sequence in the music video shows Grant sitting on a couch in a shadowy room; the main source of illumination is a TV screen that emits radiant blue light. Grant stands up, takes a step, and promptly sinks through the floor with a splash. The living room floor was still, dark water. Although Grant was black and the song was about a recent black uprising in Brixton, a primarily black Caribbean district in London, the arresting and abstract imagery of the music video was the hook. Accordingly, MTV's need for entertaining and visually interesting programming made "Electric Avenue" a programming staple, which also provided a fleeting moment of black racial diversity in MTV's all-white programming.

Likewise, the black British reggae group Musical Youth achieved MTV airplay with their mega-hit single "Pass the Dutchie" (1982). The group consisted of five young black boys singing and playing all their instruments. Arguably, Musical Youth garnered MTV airplay as a British reggae version of the African American pop group the Jackson 5. The video showcased the cuteness of the youngest member of the group by focusing on him singing. Yet "Pass the Dutchie" was not merely a cute novelty act. The song spoke to the impact of recessionary pressures on Britain's black population in the throes of 1980s Thatcherism, a point playfully alluded to by having the five boys perform in a British court. In the long run, the need for videos to fill the twenty-four-hour programming requirements of the fledgling music video station helped bring songs such as "Electric Avenue" and "Pass the Dutchie" to the foreground and placed European racial politics in the background.

During the early 1980s racially integrated bands, such as The Specials and Culture Club, also contributed to creating deeper fissures in the structured absence of blackness at MTV and helped undermine MTV's strident Jim Crow programming. The optics of racially integrated bands playing British new wave pop songs on the emergent music channel helped to destabilize the erroneous notion and prevailing racial politics of the American music industry that black artists play only R&B music. Accordingly, with the release of *1999* Prince was in an auspicious position to capitalize on the optic leeway MTV exhibited for exotic black performers, novel black music groups, and racially diversified bands that did not play R&B music. Prince's *1999* double album was poised to take advantage of this leeway given that Prince was literally making music that defied racial categorization. But how could he capitalize on his unique sonic pedigree in a visual medium? Prince's music video for "1999" was the answer.

The "1999" video was light-years from the one-man-band special effects presented in the music video for "I Wanna Be Your Lover." The latter presented multiple versions of Prince simultaneously playing various instruments and underscored the optic centrality of Prince, almost to a fault. In comparison, the video for "1999" was all about placing Prince on the periphery and highlighting diversity. At first blush, the "1999" video covered familiar visual ground. Prince and his band performed in a closed soundstage, and a fog machine generated ambient atmosphere, a setup seen in the "Dirty Mind," "Controversy," and "Sexuality" videos. But "1999" was different. Not in location but in how the video was edited. In particular, Bruce Gower's direction for "1999" was more visually encompassing than that of previous Prince music videos, and the editing underscored the racial diversity of the band. Case in point, the beginning of the video presents multiple montage shots and freeze frames of Prince's white band mates and calls attention to the fact that the seven-member band consists of more white members than blacks (four whites and three African Americans). Most important, prolonged attention is given to two dissimilar white female members playing the same keyboard.

The female duo consisted of Jill Jones, a bob-cut, peroxide-dyed blonde sporting a nautical captain's hat cocked to the side, and Lisa Coleman, a long-haired brunette delivering her best "bedroom eyes" to the camera. With their cheek-to-cheek singing style and synchronized close dancing, their performance hinted at an intimate relationship between the two, and their seductive gaze into the camera was a nonverbal invitation to the viewer to join them. Without a doubt, the "1999" video fixated on the optic foreplay of Jones and Coleman staring seductively into the camera, even going so far as to insert and superimpose the image of the two women singing cheek-to-cheek above the entire band as Prince sings.

The lipstick lesbianism intimated by Jones and Coleman catered to male sexual fantasy. Most importantly, Jones and Coleman redirected sexual impulses and anxieties created by the presence of an androgynous black man onto them. Accordingly, the video promoted the sexual tension and sexual allure of two white women as the visual centerpiece of the video and not Prince, a point signaled by the freeze frame special effect of the pair placed above the stage. The visual optics of white inclusion with the "1999" video went way beyond snagging a gig at a local dancehall or community center in Minneapolis. The inclusion of white band members performed significant symbolic work by making both Prince and his music crossover friendly enough to garner national cable television exposure on MTV. The music video for "1999" was not the only site that optically displaced Prince. Unlike the previous four LP covers that prominently placed a picture of Prince on the cover, Prince was nowhere to be found on the front or back cover of the *1999* album. Individually, these factoids are interesting tidbits but the sum of these visual cues signal *1999* was situated to transcend the discriminatory hurdles MTV erected for black artists in the early 1980s.

1999 also saw Prince modifying his punk pedigree by fully embracing the nascent flair of new wave's new romanticism. The new romantic movement

"1999" (1982) video still of Jill and Lisa

stressed visual style and cropped up in London, England, alongside the emergent new wave music scene around the club scene of the late 1970s to early 1980s.[19] Early in his career Prince was a cross-dressing singer. Moreover, and most notably, Prince adopted the harsh pose of a sexual outlaw by wearing black panties under an oversized trench coat on the *Dirty Mind* release. Prince abandoned these strident sexual optics with *1999* and opted for signature elements associated with the new romantic aesthetic, a look that included frilly shirts, lace accents, makeup, a generous application of thick eyeliner, mascara, and wearing colorful clothes.[20] In Prince's case, a sparkly purple trench coat became his signature fashion statement. Various critics viewed Prince's colorful purple trench coat and frilly flop shirt style through the psychedelic prism of black rock god Jimi Hendricks's hippie stylishness or asserted that Prince copped his stylistic cues from the Beatles during their *Sgt. Pepper's Lonely Hearts Club Band* (1967) phase.[21] To the contrary, at this juncture, Prince is not making any overtures to psychedelic rock (that would come later). With "1999" Prince was just beginning to fine-tune his image around the emergent new romanticism of the 1980s, a style best showcased in the music video for the track, "Little Red Corvette."

In the "Little Red Corvette" video Prince sports his version of the quiff (the stock hairstyle of the new romantics with ample hair on top that dimin-

"1999" (1982) video still, overhead freeze frame image

ishes on the sides and back of the head), dressed in his signature purple trench coat, complemented by a white blouse with a ruffled front and body-hugging pants paired with high-heeled boots. With this new look, Prince dramatically put to rest the red and black color motif associated with new wave fashion, a signature style of Dez Dickerson, the charismatic sideman in The Revolution. Dez's look was still in line with the new wave motif. For the "1999" video he wore a white headband emblazoned with the red Hino-maru symbol on the front, an imperial emblem of Japan's "rising sun." He also rocked a two-toned red and black fitted jumpsuit. For Prince, however, the red and black color scheme was passé.

Prince's shift in style also dovetailed with his proclivity for melodramatic emoting when performing for the camera. Sure Prince was guilty of over-projecting facial expressions on the "Little Red Corvette" video, but his melodramatic mugging for the camera made for a commanding and char-ismatic "new romantic" performance. In addition, "Little Red Corvette" video provided the perfect visual touch to complement Prince's doe-eyed romantic expressions and performance pageantry. The stage was bathed in a red glow from red floodlights. Through this scarlet prism, a moody visual ambience was created that accentuated Prince's red-light district bump and grind dancing interlude where he prances about, aggressively sways his hips,

"Little Red Corvette" (1982) video still, Prince's new romantic look

and displays a range of dance moves. Prince was also well served by the musicality of "Little Red Corvette" with its rock-centric arrangement and sophisticated guitar solo. As a result, "Little Red Corvette" was an AOR programmer's wet dream and reached number six on the *Billboard* pop charts, further helping Prince make deeper incursions across MTV's color barrier.

This is not to say that all of Prince's videos from the *1999* release were as fashion forward as "Little Red Corvette." For example, the music video for "Automatic" is rife with stylistic miscues. The "Automatic" music video dished out a generous dose of pop S&M, a style reminiscent of Prince from his *Dirty Mind* days. In the video Prince is stripped of his shirt, tied to the headboard of a bed, and flogged by band mates Lisa and Jill, as the guitar solo kicks into overdrive. The length of the video was just as excessive as the images. The video clocked in at nearly eight and a half minutes. "Automatic" was the type of music video, that aired early in the morning on the USA Network cable channel show *Night Flight* (1981–1988), a cult film and music video program. *Night Flight*, most likely, had more leeway to present provocative and even unedited music videos because the show aired in the late night to early morning programming slot.[22] Perhaps what contributed most to the viability of "1999" and "Little Red Corvette" as music videos worthy of constant MTV airplay was the fact that both songs were pop chart hit singles. But if the artist was black, just having a hit single was not guaranteed to compel MTV to air the video.

For instance, Rick James's "Super Freak," a hit dance track from his *Street Songs* (1981) album reached #16 on the pop chart and #3 on the R&B chart. Sonically, "Super Freak" was a new wave dance track with a distinctive up-tempo bass line augmented with a propulsive hook played on a keyboard synthesizer. The track was a new wave tour de force, at turns funky, experimental, and discordant. But it did not matter. MTV rejected playing the "Super Freak" video on its station, a decision that propelled James to publicly accuse MTV of racism.[23] James became a vocal critic of MTV and claimed that overt racism impacted him as well as a multitude of other black artists. For James, MTV unfairly shut out black artists from the marketing bonanza that MTV provided to white rock artists. Eventually James took his claims to the public and in 1983 he appeared on *Nightline*, a late-night news show, proclaiming black artists were denied airplay on MTV, except for an approved handful.

A cynical assessment of James's outrage places his criticism as a personal affront and driven by his personal stake in having access to MTV to enhance his career. Yet even an established white rock artist such as David Bowie saw the merits of James's accusation as an example of systemic racism and was compelled to take MTV to task for it. In a 1983 MTV interview Bowie challenged the MTV video DJ Mark Goodman by asking him why black artists were few and far between on the station. Despite the denials of racism by Goodman and MTV executives, MTV's embrace of Prince made Prince appear, at the least, like a token entertainer intended to represent the type of black artist and music that was acceptable to MTV, and by extension, its idealized notion of a white MTV audience. James's accusation of racism by MTV rightfully brought attention to the racially discriminatory tendencies of MTV in particular and the music industry in general. Yet, in retrospect, James's "Super Freak" video was a subpar sample to use as a clear case of racism.[24] The music video had several aesthetic issues that easily invited dismissal for consideration as a video that demands a spot in MTV's programming rotation.

The "Super Freak" video was hamstrung by low-grade film stock, a minimalist set, a dingy white backdrop, garish makeup on the female dancers, overbearing close-ups and serpentine imagery of various women writhing around James, repeatedly flicking their tongues to the camera. Basically,

"Super Freak" looked more like some type of coin-operated pornographic "loop," the kind of snippet played in sex shop arcades that littered New York City's Times Square throughout the 1970s. Admittedly, the video captured the bacchanalian quality of James's lifestyle. In addition, the optic energy in the "Super Freak" video clearly underscores James's hyperheterosexuality. The camera constantly focuses on a variety of women simultaneously pawing at James and James coveting them in return. Most likely any racism directed toward the video had to do with the racial and sexual anxiety "Super Freak" easily stoked by showing James as an object of desire for white women and placing their desire in the foreground of the video.

In contrast, to James's "Super Freak," white female desire was redirected away from Prince in the "1999" music video. The sexual tension circulating in the "1999" music video was between the two white women dancing with each other, not the black guy in the purple trench coat. On "Little Red Corvette" Prince also benefited from his overt use of androgyny to reinforce a doe-eyed, effeminate Lothario look, a visual cue that Prince was a foil to the red-blooded, all-American (read white) heterosexual male. This effeminate style and manner signaled that Prince did not have a stake in America's patriarchal order and popular imagining(s) of "manhood." With the "Super Freak" video James blatantly symbolized a black heterosexual satyr constantly in pursuit of white women, an image that invoked centuries-old racial anxieties regarding race and sex. In America, interracial sexuality is fraught with violence and instances of severe censure imposed on the black body, ranging from lynching, Jack Johnson and the Mann Act, the "Scottsboro Boys" case, the tortured death of Emmett Till to the horror film *Get Out* (2017). With "Super Freak" James's formula for representing male black sexuality invited stiff resistance as a viable video for predominantly white MTV executives, their assumed audience, and their stilted research.[25] Consequently, regardless of James's aesthetic miscues his claims of racism were warranted.

Perhaps the racially integrated optics of Prince's band, which had more whites than blacks, gave the impression that Prince better fit the narrow notions of what type of black artist could reap valuable exposure on MTV. As it stood, even Prince's black R&B side projects included white band members. Vanity 6 included Brenda Bennett, a white woman singing alongside two black women. The Time had Monte Moir, a white keyboardist, and later, when Morris Day left the group, the band was remade with a white male and a white woman as bandleaders. At best, Prince purposefully constructed his bands and side projects to, literally, represent music that defied strident racial groupings. Nonetheless, there was still something complicit and contrived about the racially integrated optics of Prince's band and his various side projects. At worst, such racial modifications reeked of a cynical choice to appeal to a white audience and cultivate crossover appeal, a formula that portended Prince valued whites more than blacks. Either way, racial diversity was a cornerstone of Prince's sound and image. Prince said as much about racial diversity in a *Rolling Stone* interview where he candidly admitted, "There was a lot of pressure from my ex-buddies in other bands not to have white members in the band. But I always wanted a band that was black and white. Half the musicians I knew only listened to one type of music. That wasn't good enough for me."[26]

No matter which side you chose, Prince offered a form of racial optics that incorporated real racial diversity with his band along with the broad range of musical styles he recorded. Even the name, The Revolution signaled the music, the band, and its lead figure were about transformation, cultural independence, sexual nonconformity, and racial freedom. Ostensibly, Prince's inclusion of whites in his groups appeared tailor made to meet the visual appeasement MTV seemed to require for musicians to earn a spot in their programming rotation, and, without a doubt, Prince's "white" pop-oriented tracks were the ones that slipped past MTV's color line and made it into MTV's rotation. In reality, the more mechanical attempt at generating crossover appeal to breech MTV's Jim Crow video programming was not Prince, it was Michael Jackson, with his monumental, record-shattering release *Thriller* (1982).

Keep in mind that before *Thriller* Michael Jackson was firmly situated as the centerpiece of an all-black group called the Jackson 5. Although Jackson released crossover-hit singles as the lead singer of the group on a variety of studio releases between 1972 and 1975, the crossover success of the Jackson 5 was, on the whole, a product of the marketing strategies of Motown records.[27] Most importantly, after departing Motown, Jackson established his solo artist credentials firmly rooted in the R&B tradition by releasing *Off the Wall* (1979), a dance-record masterpiece that blended disco grooves with jazz textures. Consequently, *Off the Wall* was not a crossover success, even though it garnered critical and commercial success as a megahit release. *Off the Wall* was awarded numerous accolades as a black album, and Jackson gained recognition as an outstanding black artist. *Thriller* was Michael Jackson's follow-up to *Off the Wall* and was consciously constructed in a manner to avoid a repeat of the racial pigeonholing of the latter. To this purpose, *Thriller* boasted the inclusion of various white performers—the voice of Vincent Price on the title track, a duet with iconic Beatle member Paul McCartney on the "Girl Is Mine," and the inclusion of an astounding guitar solo on "Beat It," played by rock guitar hero Eddie Van Halen.

Prince was more organic than Jackson in cultivating a crossover career. For example, Prince did not require white *guest stars* to court a crossover audience because he was several years deep in promoting a racially integrated band and perfecting his hybrid, white new wave meets black funk music (i.e., the "Minneapolis sound"). With *Thriller* Jackson courted white music consumers in a blatant and mechanical manner. In addition, CBS records strongarmed MTV executives into putting Jackson's videos on the air with threats against the music station of an economic boycott by the record company.[28] Corporate advocacy along with popular taste led to the music videos "Billie Jean," "Beat It," and "Thriller" eventually gaining exposure on MTV. Shortly after getting his videos on MTV, Jackson's music and image became a crossover staple of MTV programming, and, almost overnight, Jackson morphed from being a black artist into a pop icon the world was compelled to listen and dance to. In the end, Jackson's *Thriller* made extraordinary incursions into MTV's video programming and became the best-selling record of all time.

In contrast, Prince's *1999* LP, as well as the videos for "1999" and "Little Red Corvette," were sure-footed continuations of a rock, new wave–inflected sound, look, and crossover sensibility already expressed on Prince's four previous releases leading up to *1999*. In so doing, Prince challenged the marginalization of black music, as only played by black people for black people, by creating a "new" style of black music. Prince's music was an alternative and innovative space of sonic and racial elasticity, whereby a black artist, fluent in traditional R&B music, could create a more innovative and experimental soundscape for the development of future musical genres. Go back and listen to "Annie Christian" (*Controversy*) and you hear the early building blocks for house music, Detroit techno, and even the electro-funk hiphop of "Planet Rock." Moreover, despite MTV's embrace of Prince's growing pop appeal as a crossover artist, Prince did not forsake the black aesthetic or his black audience.

For example, traditional R&B slow jams are interspersed throughout Prince's discography along with various B-side tracks. Like Barry White, Al Green, Minnie Riperton, and Teddy Pendergrass, just to name a few, Prince provided his black listeners with first-rate "baby making music." The *Controversy* release contained the R&B slow jam "Do Me Baby," a soulful, sultry, falsetto-laced ballad that alternatively aches of brash desire and seductive whispers articulated across gospel-inflected piano riffs. *1999* offered "International Lover," a slow jam that mimicked the rhythmic crescendo and denouement of intercourse itself. For B-side aficionados the standout slow jam was "How Come You Don't Call Me Anymore," a heavy blues piano–based lament over lost love. Consequently, Prince's initial responsiveness to new wave as a sonic blueprint for modifying his own sound did not eliminate a black R&B music sensibility. Had Prince continued exploring this new wave sensibility he could have contributed to further reframing the parameters of the genre around race and mainstream achievement.

Ultimately, Prince's MTV music videos had the most transformative impact for moving Prince from an obscure cross-dressing musician from Minneapolis, Minnesota, to a mainstream pop star. Without a doubt, the "1999" and "Little Red Corvette" videos altered the racial optics of MTV and made the cable station's informal color barrier more porous for subsequent African American artists to slip into. After *1999* Prince turned up the visual intensity of his newfound romantic style several notches by wearing lace and frilly pirate shirts in his hugely successful film *Purple Rain* (1984). The soundtrack proved even more successful than *1999* and the music more radical. Prince did not include a bass line on the song "When Doves Cry," a number one smash single from the film's soundtrack. Notwithstanding the phenomenal breakthrough success of *Purple Rain*, the film also provided a spate of racial miscues that betrayed the best of the broadminded racial politics Prince and his band originally symbolized.

The film *Purple Rain* reanimated the well-worn racial cliché of the tragic mulatto, a biracial black person that is melancholy and most often alienated or estranged from blackness and desirous of white acceptance and legitimacy.[29] In fact, during Prince's *Purple Rain* phase he even claimed he was half white when he wasn't.[30] Consequently, with *Purple Rain* Prince betrayed his yearning for the type of racial utopia expressed on the song "Uptown," a place where "Good times were rolling / white, black, Puerto Rican / Everybody just a-freakin." Instead, by Prince embracing the figure of a tragic mulatto, to paraphrase another stanza from "Uptown," Prince conveyed he was a "little mixed up [dude] . . . a victim of society and all its pains."

3

Enfant Terrible

*We are having financial troubles and
that's because we're not getting the
crossover bucks. We are not getting the
white folk money. Most of our money
comes from the minorities around the
world and, although there are a lot of
them, they don't have as much as one rich
white person.*
—Reverend James L. White (Richard
Pryor), *The Richard Pryor Show*

Purple Rain, Prince's semiautobiographical movie, premiered in the summer of 1984 and became a crossover box-office sensation. For a guy that had been booed off the stage only three years earlier, after a humiliating and truncated performance as the opening act for the *Rolling Stones*, it seemed almost impossible Prince would have a successful film made about his life. Remarkably, *Purple Rain* was a hit movie and grossed nearly seven times its bare-bones seven million dollar production budget. In addition, the accompanying album, also entitled *Purple Rain*, spent twenty-four weeks as the number one album on the *Billboard* Top 200 charts (achieving platinum

status thirteen times over). The release of the film and soundtrack simultaneously provided Prince with a number one movie, a number one album,
and a number one song.[1] Moreover, Prince fans, new and old, were not the
only ones praising his film and music. From the critics, the film snagged a
couple of prestigious awards; an Oscar for Best Music/Original Song Score
and a Grammy for the score. Without a doubt, the most obvious observation is that *Purple Rain* was Prince's crowning crossover achievement, and
it propelled him into the rarified strata of an American pop cultural icon.
Acclaimed music journalist Allen Light, in the fun fact-filled book, *Let's
Go Crazy: Prince and the Making of Purple Rain* (2014), breathes new life
into these amazing accomplishments and draws a compact portrait of Prince
and the social environment of the era.

Light's book details a series of mundane, noteworthy, and obscure occur-
rences concerning Prince's semiautobiographical movie. One particular,
almost minuscule element from his book was most fascinating to me, a prescreening of the film just prior to the official release of *Purple Rain*. Light
writes this about the event:

> Warner Bros. may have been convinced to release *Purple Rain*, but they still
> didn't really know what it was (and they still had not determined whether
> they were going to put their name on it or not). The next order of business
> was to see how a real audience responded. The studio set up a screening in
> Culver City, California, an area that could produce a multiracial crowd. . . .
> They showed the movie in a big theater, with a capacity of six hundred or so.
> The young audience went wild watching the film. Afterward, following the
> usual protocol, they filled out cards that offered their scores on different
> aspects of the movie. What came back were, according to Cavallo, the best
> numbers Warner's could remember ever seeing.[2]

Light's writing about the test screening is, for the most part, uneventful, a
small detail contributing to a greater mosaic of meaning that tallies the success of the film at various stages. For me, however, Light's prescreening
recap is monumental. Why? I was there in the audience that night, a young
teenager excited to see a film starring one of my favorite musicians.

At the time of this writing, the *Purple Rain* test screening was more than
three decades ago, and the exact dates and details are somewhat foggy. But
several facts remain vivid to this day. I was a freshman at Culver City High
School and already quite familiar with Prince as a ninth grader because of

Harold, a high-flying basketball opponent of mine. We were also friends when I lived in Hawthorne, California. I recall before (or was it after?) playing a game of one-on-one basketball Harold referenced Prince when he recounted one of his sexual exploits. I seldom trusted anything Harold declared when it concerned sex. We bonded over hoops and hip-hop. Both of us were fans of "The Message" (1982), by Grandmaster Flash and the Furious Five. The most Prince music I heard, or cared to take the time to listen to then, was the radio airplay given to "Let's Work," a black dance groove that was popular with my middle school peers. Prince was cool enough but I was into exploring the new music coming out of the grimiest sections of Bronx, New York. I liked the Funky 4 + 1 with their hit "That's the Joint" (1980) and playing Grand Mixer D.St. & The Infinity Rappers' 12-inch single "The Grand Mixer Cuts It Up" (1982), a horror movie soundtrack meets computer funk hip-hop cult classic. Nonetheless, I decided to find out for myself what Prince had to say about sex.

I copped the cassette tape version of *Dirty Mind* and my mind was blown. *Dirty Mind* affirmed Prince was not just dirty he was "nasty," a word my grandmother used to underscore something she found particularly deplorable. Incest, fellatio, pimping, bisexual cuckold threesomes, and proclamations of the virtues of giving and getting "head" made Prince the ultimate sexual outlaw. Soon after hearing *Dirty Mind* I purchased *1999* to prove I had caught up to Harold's hipness. *1999* was filled with sexual antics too. On the track "Let's Pretend We're Married" I heard Prince declare he wanted "to fuck the taste out" of a woman's mouth, and on "All the Critics Love U in New York," he confessed to "definitely masturbating." Playing Prince around the wrong people, parents in particular, would be a problem. Prince was Walkman-and-headphone-only type music.

Thanks to Harold, by the time I entered Culver High I had purchased all of Prince's previous releases and had two *1999* cassettes (because sound quality on the first deteriorated from playing it so much), had bought all The Time material (which even then I found eerily evocative of Prince), and discovered my fantasy woman was the lead singer for a group called Vanity 6. Consequently, when news started circulating around my high school of a preview of a Prince film showing at a nearby studio, of course, I was going to be there. I told my mother I was going, after basketball practice, with some of my teammates to an advance screening of a Prince movie. On our walk to the screening, my three basketball buddies and I joked about how a Prince film was probably a porno flick.

When we arrived at what was then the inside parking lot of the studio the line was extremely long. We recognized some girls from our school camped out near the front of the line and planned to make a more formal introduction when it began to move. When the line started to stir, some older and tougher teenagers jumped in and we did the same, scooting right behind them. I don't recall the viewing space seating six hundred people, but it was wall-to-wall crowded. I do remember a spokesperson addressing the packed theater to inform us that we were not viewing the final edited version of the film; a point he conveyed by making us aware that background dubs for various crowd scenes had not been fully completed. Later in the film I saw a shot of a black patron whistling his approval after a band performed, but there was no sound of him whistling. I remember thinking, "Yeah, that's what the spokesperson meant." Despite an assortment of obscure sound-editing omissions the dialogue was captivating, and the majority of the musical performances were spectacular.

At the conclusion of the film the spokesperson informed the audience to fill out a card-questionnaire concerning what we thought about the film. I was more eager to talk to my friends about the movie, not jot my thoughts down like I was taking a creative-writing exam. Nevertheless, I hurriedly scribbled down "More Morris Day." During our walk to the bus stop and our wait for the bus to arrive, and then throughout the short ride to our respective drop-off points, we gave *Purple Rain* the type of rigorous analysis the studio executives were trying to glean with their questionnaire. The consensus of my peer group, consisting of four African American high school basketball-playing males between the ages of fourteen and sixteen, was this: Prince was a punk, Appolonia (Patricia Kotero) was "finer than a muther-fucker," Morris should have won in the end, the music was good, and we all wanted to see *Purple Rain* again. To say the least, in the wake of that advance screening, *Purple Rain* left an indelible visual and sonic impression on me. The music was a perfect match for the snapshot images of the film I had committed to memory; the opening montage, the synchronized dancing of The Time, Apollonia riding on the back of Prince's purple motorcycle down a countryside road, and the moody finale of Prince proclaiming "I never meant to cause you any sorrow / I never meant to cause you any pain."

When the film finally came out I did see it again and again. I estimate at least five times. By then all the sound-editing flubs were fixed, and the music sounded progressively louder, especially when I went to see the film on a Friday or Saturday night in Westwood Village, a commercial and primetime people-watching district within short walking distance of UCLA. I can't speak to the number of repeat viewings of the film that contributed to the box office achievement and cultural impact of *Purple Rain*, but I venture to say that repeated viewings were a significant factor for the box office success of the film. In retrospect, how throngs of young teenagers were allowed to view an advanced screening of an R-rated film escapes me now. Moreover, I don't recall how my friends and I were able to repeatedly view the film after the official release. Maybe because my basketball friends and I were tall and looked older we could pass muster at the ticket booth, or maybe not. Nonetheless, it seemed like every showing was packed with teenagers alongside numerous young adults.

The album dropped just over a month before the film premiered (June 25, 1984) and delivered three top 10–charting songs; "When Doves Cry," "Let's Go Crazy," and the title track "Purple Rain." In addition, the music video for the smash hit "When Doves Cry" included snippets of footage from the upcoming film release. Accordingly, the anticipation for the film was stoked by Prince's growing musical achievement and constant MTV rotation. As a consequence of the sequential marketing, the film looked less like a film and more like an extended music video interrupted by a threadbare narrative and mediocre acting (often taking place around an argument).[3] From the music video vantage point, *Purple Rain* is just the visual embodiment of Prince's celebrity persona and his marketing motivations to become a pop star. Moreover, a conventional reading views the film primarily as a product of the recording industry and fails to correctly view *Purple Rain* as a product of, and in dialogue with, the history and discourses around race in American cinema.[4] A more accurate assessment of *Purple Rain* must situate its filmic and cultural significance within the long and dubious lineage of black racial representation in American cinema in general, and the Hollywood musical genre in particular.

Given that the birth of Hollywood cinema began with D. W. Griffith's racist masterpiece *Birth of a Nation* (1915), wherein members of the Ku Klux Klan are presented as heroic figures, for a while, the safest genre for black representation to crop up in was in film musicals. *The Jazz Singer* (1927), the first motion picture to fuse sound with film, (re)presented the American theatrical performance of blackface on screen, whereby white performers in makeup presented comedic, stereotypical, and overly emotive portrayals of black folk to entertain white audiences.[5] *The Jazz Singer* kept the nineteenth-century minstrel tradition insulated and persevered well into the twentieth century by having the star of the film, Al Jolson, perform his signature song "My Mammy" in blackface. Eventually, the Hollywood musical genre would enlist real black people to sing and dance in front of the camera. Nonetheless, the stereotypical representations of black folk did not abate. Hollywood film musicals such as *Hallelujah* (1929) and *Hearts in Dixie* (1929) boasted all-black casts and still delivered a shrill reinforcement of black racial stereotypes.[6]

Despite the dubious placement and the stereotypical constraints placed on black performers during the inception of the American film musical the genre was almost a progressive space for black representation. In fact, during the 1930s through the 1950s, Hollywood devised an ingenious method to best capitalize on the off-screen popularity of black entertainers in their music-dominated features. Film historian Donald Bogle best explains this filmic formula for black racial representation in early American cinema: "As the Negro performers grew in popularity, there evolved a special platform for displaying the entertainer to his best advantage . . . producers introduced specific musical interludes in which the [black] entertainer could perform unhampered by a storyline. Frequently, a nightclub scene was introduced into the movie so that the [black] performer would have a natural setting. The interludes were casually inserted in the films. . . . The entertainer would provide a dazzling interlude and then fade from the scene, leaving the plot to continue without him [/her]."[7] For several decades, when it came to black representation in American cinema, the "musical production number" was the go-to plan for showcasing popular black performers. The film career of Bill "Bojangles" Robinson is a testimony to this formula. Robinson was an extremely talented tap dancer in his own right, but he became crossover famous in a succession of four films released in the late 1930s by dancing with a little white girl named Shirley Temple.

In due course, the Hollywood film industry started casting all-black musicals. The aesthetic experiment was a mixed bag of successes and failures. There was the star-studded standout *Stormy Weather* (1943), the well-intentioned *Cabin in the Sky* (1943), the dubious dreck of *Song of the South* (1946), the extravagant *Carmen Jones* (1954), and the bloated misfire *Porgy and Bess* (1959). By the early 1960s, however, images of happy, singing black people appeared patently false against the backdrop of real-world images of black people attacked by dogs and blasted by water hoses in their push for racial equality during the cresting Civil Rights movement. Against this somber sociopolitical setting, a variety of films addressing social problems cropped up—*A Raisin in the Sun* (1961), *A Patch of Blue* (1965), and *Guess Who's Coming to Dinner* (1967)—that tackled ongoing racial issues plaguing American society. By the early 1970s social problem films morphed into blaxploitation cinema that offered strident formulaic representations of militant Black Power politics. Moreover, like the social problems film era that preceded it, blaxploitation cinema had no room for black musicals, even though music was a cornerstone of the genre thanks to Melvin Van Peeble's pioneering blaxploitation film *Sweet Sweetback's Baadasssss Song* (1971). The film made the soundtrack a central part of the story and served as a paradigm for subsequent blaxploitation films to imitate.[8]

Arguably, the film that best epitomized the centrality of music for the blaxploitation genre is *Shaft* (1971). The opening credits of *Shaft* play like the prototype for contemporary black music videos. The film begins with a propulsive wa-wa guitar rhythm and high-hat percussion playing in the background as private detective John Shaft (Richard Roundtree) stalks the dingy streets of New York City with an air of aristocratic cool. Perhaps *Superfly* (1972) is the only other blaxploitation film to rival the beginning of *Shaft*, with its four-minute cocaine distribution montage set to Curtis Mayfield's track "Pusher Man." The montage consists of a series of still photos, presented with a split-screen effect, depicting how cocaine goes from a black dealer to white working- and middle-class professionals in search of a good time. Ultimately, *Shaft* and *Superfly* delivered soundtracks that proved just as popular and sonically significant as the films. As a result, almost as a rule of thumb, blaxploitation films were committed to creating a popular score to market the film and generate profit by selling a successful soundtrack. Frequently, a strong soundtrack buoyed dead-weight narratives; a trend exemplified by films such as *Sparkle* (1976), *Car Wash* (1976), and, to a lesser extent, *The Wiz* (1978).

By the early 1980s blaxploitation had fallen flat and was no longer a dominant box-office presence. Ironically, in the genre's wake, a refurbished version of the movie musical surfaced as the most viable medium to showcase emergent black styles and cultural expressions. For example, the slick postmodern, music-centric film *Flashdance* (1983) shoehorned hip-hop dancing into its odd narrative about a full-time female welder and part-time exotic dancer aiming for admittance to a prestigious dance conservatory. The film was a visually groundbreaking bona fide box office success. Dynamic dance sequences, captivating visuals, and a popular soundtrack negated weak acting chops and a mediocre plot.

Arguably, *Purple Rain* benefited from the same aesthetic impulses circulating throughout the music video era of the early 1980s. In this sense, *Purple Rain* was a great example of a film in sync with a public yearning for more music-video-meets-film mash-ups similar to *Flashdance*. Both films presented self-contained music performance set pieces, kinetic visuals, and colorful stage routines to propel the narrative of the film. Certainly, *Purple Rain* greatly benefited from the sheer power of a platinum-selling soundtrack and made-for-crossover-film surprise success. Yet lurking below the surface of *Purple Rain*'s minimal narrative was a complex ideology concerned with establishing a symbolic polarity between a white racial orientation and a black racial identity. In *Purple Rain* racial blackness is coded as violent, demeaning, harsh, judgmental, and unsuccessful, whereas whiteness is coded as sincere, forgiving, gracious, and successful. This racial dichotomy permeates *Purple Rain*, yet race is never mentioned in the film regarding the principal characters, their backgrounds, or their bands.

Ostensibly, *Purple Rain* is a film about two aspiring bands pitted against one another for the privilege of earning band headliner status at the First Avenue nightclub, a venue known for launching headliner groups into the music industry. The first five minutes of *Purple Rain* brilliantly present this competitive dichotomy and capture the main characters' traits and their backstage machinations with a fast-moving, nonlinear montage of the two rival bandleaders making their respective way to the performance venue. "The Kid" (Prince Rogers Nelson) is a sullen misunderstood musician and bandleader of The Revolution. Morris (Morris Day) is the charismatic front man for The Time. The two bandleaders not only compete over who will vanquish the other but they also find themselves pursuing the same romantic interest in the film, a vivacious young woman and fledgling singer named Apollonia (Patricia Kotero).

The visual rhetoric of the film's opening also establishes a racial dichotomy between the rival characters. The Kid is shown applying makeup and eyeliner to his face in preparation for his performance. Shots of The Kid's face are intercut with a rapid montage of extreme close-ups of various white club spectators. The quick succession of shots signals a clear connection between The Kid and the various white club-goers wearing garish face paint. In contrast, as The Time performs the song "Jungle Love," black attendees are primarily shown, and, as if this were not enough of a visual cue, as The Time performs, a shot of five black men performing a synchronized dance routine underscores their corresponding racial appeal.

Simply stated, The Time is the black band that appeals to a black audience, whereas The Revolution is a predominantly white band that appeals to a white audience.[9] In addition, the film constantly telegraphs to the viewing audience which side is problematic and the correct racial orientation to pick.

In *Purple Rain* racial "blackness" is often underscored by a variety of unsettling atmospherics that borrow from the horror film genre. For example, The Kid's home is repeatedly presented as the source of dread and haunting danger, a point underscored by the use of strange ambient sounds and the manner by which the interior home scenes emphasize shadows and dark silhouettes.[10] Moreover, The Kid's black father, Francis (Clarence William III), symbolizes the violent "monster" waiting behind the door and occupying the shadows inside their home. This visual scheme is first introduced to the viewing audience when The Kid returns home from a club performance and fearfully pauses at the door, listening to his father verbally attacking his white mother.

The Kid charges through the door to discover his father has pinned his mother into a corner and is screaming at her and attempts to separate the two. Francis responds with a brutalizing slap that knocks The Kid to the floor. Francis glares at him as he lies on the floor, stunned, while the mother stands in the background with a look of cowed distress. Francis is most often depicted as a solitary, violent, and intimidating figure that asserts his domineering presence in the domestic space of the home where he exerts physical abuse against his wife (Olga Karlatos) and his son. The abusive scene sets the stage for placing The Kid, literally, at the center of two antagonistic polarities, his black father and black masculinity on one side and his white mother and white femininity on the other.

The Kid's basement room further visually underscores this racialized use of gender in the film. The Kid's room is decorated like a curio boutique, with various delicate white figurines, Pierrot dolls, and candles placed throughout the space. Adorning the walls and mirror of his basement room are numerous Patrick Nagel–like facial sketches of expressionless white women with dark hair. This aesthetic theme culminates in an oversized painted mural of a white woman with a blank stare covering an entire wall.[11] Ostensibly, the use of white dolls, along with adorning his walls with white women, symbolically functions to assert The Kid's feminine sensibility and gender fluidity. To this point and without a doubt, gender politics stands in the forefront of the film and provides a wealth of ideological fodder for

Morris faces Prince in *Purple Rain* (1984), a contrast of attitude and style.

analysis.[12] But the excessive deployment of the feminine also speaks to race. There are no black dolls or black women adorning any wall space in that basement. Racially speaking, The Kid's room is a strident articulation of whiteness vis-à-vis the structured absence of blackness. In this way, such imagery is as much about race as it is about gender.

In contrast to the interior, subterranean, serene, and pretty world of whiteness that The Kid has constructed in the basement of his parents' house, the outside world, like the maniacal black father that lives above him, is chaotic and violent. Morris, the other significant male black antagonist in the film, repeatedly refers to women as bitches and is violently demeaning toward women, a point highlighted when Morris commands his manservant Jerome (Jerome Benton) to throw a woman into a trash bin in broad daylight for reprimanding him in public. Both father and foe overlap in their palpable animosity and disrespect of women. As a result, black male sexuality is presented as a destructive and dehumanizing manifestation in *Purple Rain*. In this sense, racial blackness is saddled with a variety of negative attributes. Francis and Morris not only represent maniacal masculinity but also pathological blackness.

In *Purple Rain* music is also used to make a racial distinction and reaffirm the racially dichotomous choice The Kid faces, an option first set up by the argument between his father and mother. Billy, the owner of the First Avenue club, chastises The Kid for being like his father and playing music that is too weird, too personal, and has no broad-based appeal. In this manner, Francis embodies a brooding, self-destructive, and insular musician, a point telegraphed in a scene where The Kid rushes home, after finding his mother crying on the sidewalk, to confront Francis for beating her. Shortly after entering the home he hears Francis playing a beautiful melody on the piano. Struck by the haunting tune he calmly asks about seeing his father's compositions. Francis responds with a curt statement, "No man, I don't write them down. I don't have to. That's the big difference between you and me."

Despite his father's declaration, The Kid is marked as being similar to his abusive father. Earlier in the film, The Kid violently slaps his budding love interest in a fit of rage and repeatedly spurns attempts by Wendy (Wendy Melvion) and Lisa (Lisa Coleman), his white female band members, to collaborate. Francis gives the impression he is only concerned with his own wants, the demands he makes of his wife, and the interior dialogue of his music shut off from the world. The Kid can either choose his father's solitary, troubled, and detached demeanor or break ranks with the maniacal masculinity of his father by collaborating on a song with Wendy and Lisa. Not surprisingly, in order to forge a new and triumphant pop persona The Kid embraces a collaborative stance with Wendy and Lisa, marked by expressive emotional intimacy on stage when they perform the song "Purple Rain." At the conclusion of the song The Kid gives a watery-eyed Wendy a delicate kiss on the cheek, signaling he has clearly broken ranks from the maniacal masculinity and pathological blackness epitomized by Francis.[13] But The Kid's acquiescence to the feminine also entails his transcendence of blackness. The visual rhetoric of The Kid's climactic "Purple Rain" performance amplifies not only the triumphant power of whiteness but the role of racial blackness in legitimizing The Kid's racially transcendent crossover pop persona.

Before The Kid performs "Purple Rain," reaction shots and corresponding close-ups of white concertgoers are shown. This pattern is disrupted by shots of several solemn black men interspersed throughout the predominantly white audience staring at the stage. As the performance progresses, a succession of close-up shots show the black men in the audience nodding their heads in approval. The general point of the scene clearly conveys how the black attendees, scattered among the predominantly white audience, express their approval and grant The Kid permission to proceed in this new direction. Moreover, the climactic "Purple Rain" and subsequent demand by the predominantly white audience for an encore performance permit The Kid to fully demonstrate his broad appeal and potential for colorblind commercial success. The encore performance of the respective pop-rock songs "I Would Die 4 U" and "Baby I'm a Star" had, at best, a facile connection to anything close to a black aesthetic. In the end, whiteness won, a victory signaled by The Kid adopting and affirming the classic masturbatory "cock-rocker" posture of a rock and roll guitarist on the closing song "Baby I'm a Star." Near the conclusion of the performance, The Kid grabs a guitar rigged to spurt water and strokes the guitar neck up and down until water erupts from his guitar and sprays the crowd.

For me, such visual antics have not held up well over time. The obligatory "money shot" seemed like a ploy to distract from a mediocre pop song. But as sexual spectacle, this contrived climax was an ingenious display of how Prince solidified his image as a rock artist, vis-à-vis the end of the film. The concluding shot signals The Kid is now a star that exudes an aura of erotic rebelliousness and a faux sense of danger commonly associated with white lead rock guitarists. On the one hand, film critic Armond White applauded *Purple Rain* for not addressing race in any manifest manner.[14] On the other hand, Nelson George, a notable music critic of the period, expressed reservations around the type of racial representation presented in *Purple Rain* and the crossover impulse it signaled. George was piqued by the way race was deployed in casting actors for *Purple Rain*. He stated, "In the quasiautobiographical film *Purple Rain*, Prince presented his mother as white, a "crossover" marketing strategy. . . . In fact, it can be argued that Prince's consistent use of mulatto and white leading ladies convinced many black male (and some female) artists to use romantic interests of similar shading in their videos, hoping to emulate Prince's success. The resulting videos seem to reinforce the stereotypic idea that dark-skinned black women are not as attractive as their light sisters."[15] For George, *Purple Rain* provided an aesthetic paradigm for subsequent black creative production, a harbinger of purposefully casting women of white or lighter complexion to cultivate a crossover viewing audience for black music video projects.

Admittedly, the female characters in *Purple Rain* appear biracial or racially ambiguous. George, however, places too much representational responsibility on Prince's narrow shoulders and overlooks the frequency of this representational trope in black films prior to *Purple Rain*. A more prudent observation recognizes that *Purple Rain* only repeated a timeworn tradition, already present in American cinema, of promoting black women with very light complexions as a source of desire and sexual wish fulfillment. Long before *Purple Rain* was ever cast Lena Horne, in the films *Cabin in the Sky* (1943) and *Stormy Weather* (1943), along with the entirety of Dorothy Dandridge's film career, are notable examples of the kind of complexion typecasting in the Hollywood film industry has a long history of promulgating. In fact, eight years prior to *Purple Rain* the film *Sparkle* (1976), a musical drama about an aspiring all-black girl group, showcased the type of racially ambiguous women of color George critiqued *Purple Rain* for fetishizing.

In *Sparkle*, the role of Sister Williams was played by Lonette McKee, a striking beauty and visual forerunner to Vanity 6 and, to a lesser extent, Patricia Kotero (aka Apollonia). Furthermore, McKee's co-star was Irene Cara, a standout beauty who had a strong resemblance to Susan Moonie, of Apollonia 6, who had a bit part in *Purple Rain*. Accordingly, George is incorrect to ascribe to Prince the fetishistic proclivities for casting black women with light complexions or ambiguously brown women in American music videos and, by extension, American cinema. This pattern has a long and involved history that preceded *Purple Rain* by decades.

What George does anticipate correctly about *Purple Rain* is how the film functions as a forerunner to constructing a crossover platform for mainstream acceptance of a black film. In order to foil the assumption or perception that two discernably black leading actors reduce a comedy, drama, or musical to merely a black film the black male lead is paired with a lead female romantic interest that is either not discernable as African American or is a Latina or in some cases a white actress. Most likely, this tactic is based on a marketing assumption that having a black man as lead and having a non–African American female as the romantic co-star aids in appealing to a broader audience and undercuts the notion that a film cast with blacks as the principal characters is a film relevant only to a black audience.

A majority of the films starring Will Smith often adopted this trope, a pattern witnessed with Salma Hayek in *Wild Wild West* (1999), Bridget Moynahan in *I, Robot* (2004), Eva Mendez in *Hitch* (2005), Alice Braga in *I Am Legend* (2007), Rosario Dawson in *Seven Pounds* (2008), Charlize

Theron in *Hancock* (2008), and Margot Robbie in *Focus* (2015). In the end, whether because of this racial formula or in spite of it, *Purple Rain* made Prince a mainstream crossover commodity, an achievement that, in many ways, emptied his persona and image of its radical potential in relation to race.[16]

Purple Rain, however, was not all negative concerning racial blackness. Admittedly, the binary demarcation between Francis and The Kid threatened to affirm the retrograde notion that black creative production dwells exclusively in the creative realm of improvisational and emotional performance and white creative expressivity reflects measured analytic thought manifest as written composition.[17] But when The Kid discovers his father's box of music, which contains numerous meticulously notated compositions written down, this revelation undercuts the strident suggestion that black creativity is purely spontaneous and natural, a point of misdirection in the film when Francis brags about not needing to write any of his music down as a point to distinguish how he is different from his son. This is the most recuperative aspect of the film concerning blackness and arguably speaks to Prince's own laborious approach to creating a grand catalog of music and tucking it away in a vault for others to progressively discover and potentially release.

Ultimately, the crossover success of *Purple Rain* set in motion a series of creative choices that amplified shortcomings not only by Prince but also for many of the principal players involved with the film. For starters, the *Purple Rain* Tour, a concert tour organized to capitalize on the success of the film, was truncated. The tour began in Detroit, Michigan, on November 4, 1984, and ended April 7, 1985, at the Orange Bowl in Miami, Florida. Prince basically called it quits in Miami, Florida, after a meager six months. On top of that, the tour never made it overseas. In addition, The Time had also come to an end. The group disbanded in the wake of the remarkable mainstream success of *Purple Rain*.

Prince was already leery of The Time outdoing him during previous tours when the charismatic Day upstaged Prince in his own film with his two-man comic chemistry opposite Jerome.[18] Like the rivals in the film, the two men became actual adversaries and fell out of favor with one another and were no longer musical co-conspirators. But it did not matter. Prince prematurely pulled the plug on his tour and contributed to the demise of The Time. *Purple Rain* had already propelled Prince into the rarified strata of a pop cultural icon. For Day it did not matter either. Day capitalized on the hype and hoopla surrounding *Purple Rain* by embarking on a semisuccessful solo musical career and enjoying a brief acting career.

Day generated a handful of banal pop-R&B dance songs, such as "Oak Tree" and "Fishnet," from respective releases *The Color of Success* (1985) and *Daydreaming* (1987). Over the long run, Day's post–*Purple Rain* career was a mixed bag. But the bigger disappointment was not Day's departure from The Time but the dulling of the racially rooted cutting edge funk sound Prince had ghost written for The Time. With the release of the group's third album, *Ice Cream Castles* (1984), their sound had grown stale with saccharin pop dance songs, such as "Jungle Love" and "The Bird." The Time was not the only Prince side project to suffer a precipitous decline in imagination and execution after *Purple Rain*. The Prince-penned new wave grooves for the *Apollonia 6* (1984) album were extremely bland, and the release fell flat. The music for the album made it immediately apparent that, as a group, Apollonia 6 was merely a contrivance for the film.

Frankly stated, Kotero could not sing or dance. A few bootlegged video performances reside on YouTube showing the girl group lip-syncing the "Sex Shooter" single.[19] The performance is uninspired, as well as awkward, and foretold that the group would soon become defunct. Even as a solo artist the result was the same for Kotero. Kotero released *Apollonia* (1988), a self-titled CD of anemic dance music that Kotero performed on *Soul Train*. The music and performance clearly confirmed acting is her strongest suit even though *Purple Rain* typecast Kotero as an exotic singing sexpot. In this sense, *Purple Rain* appeared more of an albatross than auspicious beginning for Kotero. Nevertheless, the film provided her with a stage name that would stick and furthered her acting career as a B-list actress able to sporadically pop up on television shows, such as *Falcon Crest* (1981–1990), a primetime CBS soap opera where she played "herself" as "Apollonia." With the benefit of hindsight, the full frontal nudity Kotero showed in *Purple Rain* may have overshadowed her and distracted from any thoughtful appreciation of her ability to convincingly play an ingenue in *Purple Rain*.

As the director, writer, and editor of *Purple Rain* Albert Magnoli followed his surprising success with *American Anthem* (1986), a beefcake star vehicle for Mitchell Gaylord. Mitch Gaylord played the part of a male gymnast preparing to go to the Olympics. The story was not that far from the truth given that Gaylord had recently come back from the 1984 games a breakout personality and Gold Medal winner in gymnastics. If Magnoli could transform a skinny black dude with a high voice from Minneapolis, Minnesota, from an obscure musician into a pop phenomenon then teeing off the film career of a white male Olympic Gold Medal winner was seen as having a license to print money. The film had all of Magnoli's visual ticks and narrative beats but no heart. *American Anthem* was a white version of *Purple Rain*, not in content but in structure—a famous nonactor protagonist, an authoritarian father, a big competition to prove he's a new man, and a soundtrack playing loudly during each match. Gaylord did not prove half as interesting on the parallel bars as Prince had on the stage. *American Anthem* was a dud. Magnoli went on to enjoy an anemic career as a film director but was able to accrue a more successful track record directing several of Prince's music videos after *Purple Rain*. In particular, the Sign 'o' the Times concert film is a standout example of Magnoli's job as a director.

Surprisingly, Magnoli never came close to matching the success of the film he wrote, directed, and edited. The yeoman creative labor expended on *Purple Rain* was signaled in Magnoli's directorial touch with characters like Morris, who bordered on caricature as an egotistical figure. Magnoli was able to dramatically temper the boastful front-stage veneer of Morris with moments that hinted Morris was also a sensitive and reflective figure. The first glimpse of this character trait is shown right after Apollonia rebuffs his invitation to join his new girl group. Ineffective at corralling Apollonia from the back seat of his yellow Cadillac he must chase her down and make an honest pitch that reveals a heartfelt desire to succeed. Later, Morris delivers the comment "How's the family?" as a hurtful punch line to The Kid in the wake of attempted suicide by The Kid's father. Afterward, the director shows a quiet, introspective, and visibly regretful Morris, alone in the hallway pondering his hurtful words. Short scenes such as these went a long way toward providing the pathos needed to make a seemingly one-dimensional, static character dynamic. In the end, where Day, Kotero, and Magnoli used the success of *Purple Rain* to propel their fledgling music, acting, and directorial careers, Prince actively worked to sabotage the success of *Purple Rain* and invite criticism around race with the release of his next studio album, *Around the World in a Day* (1985).

Instead of following up *Purple Rain* with a release that delivered a similar amount of pop pleasure Prince released *Around the World in a Day* (*ATWD*), a weird and impenetrable album that can clear a dance floor in an amazingly short amount of time. To Prince's credit the odd album was lauded in various circles as an intrepid artistic concept album that displayed superb musicianship.[20] The retro-psychedelic studio release rode the top of the *Billboard* chart for three weeks, an impressive accomplishment given the dearth of radio-friendly singles the LP offered. Of the nine tracks on *ATWD* only "Raspberry Beret" and "Pop Life" proved musically appealing enough to catch the ear of the audience and crack the *Billboard* top ten.[21] Without a doubt, *ATWD* was a dramatic departure from Prince's previous works, but, in retrospect, the release was more jumbled than groundbreaking, a sensibility signaled by the album cover.

For the *ATWD* album cover Prince nixed his signature doe-eyed-stare-into-the-camera pose. Instead, the cover was crammed with an assortment of weird carnival-type figures pasted onto a colorful cartoon-like jigsaw puzzle piece landscape. The visual topography did double duty as a gestalt image, a rendering of a mountain was a woman's breast and the summit was her nipple. The cover nudity, "hidden in plain sight," functioned as a subversive visual reminder of Prince's sex junkie reputation and appetite. But, for the most part, the music on *ATWD* was a hodgepodge of G-rated wistful songs filled with sitar strumming, finger cymbals, and tambourine rhythms. The eclectic instrumentality created the stark impression, upon first hearing, of a strange, unique, and daring sonic adventure. When given a deeper and more sustained listening the album's kaleidoscopic musical arrangements sounded like a hackneyed knock-off of the Beatles' *Sgt. Pepper's Lonely Hearts Club Band* (1967), a groundbreaking foray into psychedelic music and, to a lesser extent, the style of their animated film *Yellow Submarine* (1968).

The Beatles' *Sgt. Pepper's Lonely Hearts Club Band* and the Beach Boys' *Pet Sounds* (1966) rank as top-tiered pioneering examples of musicians reaching the pinnacle of artistic expression. Arguably, given the exceptional caliber of Prince's musicianship, it is not all that bewildering to anticipate Prince staking a claim, somewhere down the line, to a more challenging and experimental musical motif. Prince not only possessed exceptional music chops but also demonstrated a successful track record of mixing discordant music styles and repurposing various music genres for his own uses. As previously noted, with *Dirty Mind* through *Purple Rain*, Prince took conventional R&B elements and mixed them with new wave influences to create an innovative and propulsive synth-based musical arrangement coined the "Minneapolis sound." Accordingly, Prince's strengths were best expressed when he was distilling and extracting elements of other music genres to create his own unique sound. Even though Prince claimed *ATWD* was not taking its creative cues from the Beatles' *Sgt. Pepper's Lonely Hearts Club Band*, *ATWD* sounded more derivative than innovative, and it labored in mimicking white art rock.[22] Moreover, Prince's disavowal is difficult to accept given that Prince was prone to lying, (about his age, his racial background, and the veracity of various songs) when it suited his marketing needs.

ATWD shared too many similar elements with *Sgt. Pepper's Lonely Hearts Club Band* to accept happenstance as a reasonable explanation. With *Sgt. Pepper's Lonely Hearts Club Band* the sitars, finger symbols, and pseudo-esoteric lyrics, found on tracks like "Lucy in the Sky with Diamonds," came together to form a cohesive art-rock whole. In contrast, *ATWD* suffered from the overwrought use of these same components, a point underscored on the tracks "Condition of the Heart" and "Paisley Park." Nevertheless, *ATWD* does contain flashes of musical genius with tracks such as "Tamborine" and "Raspberry Beret." Arguably, "Raspberry Beret" is Prince's most perfect midtempo pop ballad. The song delivered a seamless mix of soulful vocals, austere acoustic guitar, and soft violin arrangements all framed by a nostalgic narrative of youthful romance. Prince even provided a tasty morsel of his signature eroticism on the track when he sings, "If I had the chance to do it all again / I wouldn't change a stroke."

The video for the track was just as interesting as the song. The "Raspberry Beret" video opened with an extended funky instrumental riff not found on the original LP release, a musical accent visually underscored by several female dancers huddled in a semicircle swaying hard to the beat. Next, Prince makes his way to the stage wearing a striking bright blue jump suit with an assortment of white clouds patterned across it, an image that evoked the dreamy romanticism of the song. Before Prince segues into the LP version of the tune he has a coughing fit, recovers, catches his breath, regains his composure, and, as if nothing happened, resumes playing. What happened? What did it mean? What was the interview-phobic Prince telling the audience through his odd actions?

After the video premiered on MTV, video deejay Mark Goodman openly contemplated what the cough meant to another guest. Prince later admitted the cynical truth, he merely "did it to be sick, to do something no one else would do."[23] Arguably, on the whole, Prince did the same with *ATWD*. Ostensibly, the release represented Prince's maverick personality on full display alongside his creative restlessness. But in Prince's confession about the affected theatrics he deployed in the video for "Raspberry Beret," one could detect a degree of contempt toward his audience. Moreover, in my mind, the obnoxious reversal of musical style on the LP made *ATWD* more of a cynical retort to the glossy pop hysteria *Purple Rain* had created around Prince and less a daring work of experimental artistry meant to make an artistic statement.

Music journalist Ronin Ro, in the aptly titled book *Prince: Inside the Music and the Masks*, contextualizes and compiles several quotes from Prince that glean a growing cynicism concerning his feelings about the growing audience he had gained because of the mega-success of *Purple Rain*:

> The album itself passed the 10 million mark. The film grossed over 70 million in the U.S. "In some ways, it was more detrimental than good," he [Prince] said in *Entertainment Weekly*. People's perception changed "and it pigeon-holed me." At concerts, kids screamed simply "because that's where the audience screamed in the movie." . . . Prince had to escape this. "I couldn't play the game," he told *Icon*. His next album—it would change all this. . . . The next album would get him away from *Purple Rain*. And he'd get it out there while this large audience—bigger than the ones that bought his earlier works—were eager to hear his next release.[24]

In light of these comments, *ATWD* was a project meant to help Prince shred to pieces the purple straitjacket fashioned, tailored and made to size out of the phenomenal pop success of *Purple Rain*.

Unfortunately, Prince further alienated his core black audience and fans that had followed him from the beginning of his career by releasing *ATWD* as a project to spite a public longing for a *Purple Rain 2* studio album. *ATWD* appeared to support previous suspicions that Prince rejected his black racial identity and catered to white musical tastes to attract a broader white rock audience.[25] As a result, *ATWD* not only exacerbated prior racial criticisms concerning Prince it also served as a thumb in the eye for new-found fans that glommed on to him because of *Purple Rain*.[26] Despite *ATWD* causing critics and fans to take pause at Prince's psychedelic sonic soundscape the album climbed the *Billboard* chart to #1 and went double platinum. Prince was so red hot that even when he offered up lukewarm material he could still heat up the music charts. Perhaps Prince's black audience may have felt alienated and left behind because of his crossover pop success with white fans due to *Purple Rain* and the art-rock disposition of *ATWD*, but Prince never abandoned his black fan base.

In fact, during the peak period of his crossover success with *Purple Rain* and alongside the *ATWD* release Prince was still delivering some of his most cutting edge music within a black music idiom. Most often his soul and funk version of his synth-based "Minneapolis sound" was on the B-sides of his mainstream singles and on a variety of new side-projects. Arguably, Prince's B-sides frequently matched, and sometimes surpassed, the innovative musicality exhibited on a variety of mainstream lead singles, a subversive oeuvre throughout his career. Tracks such as "Irresistible Bitch," "Another Lonely Christmas," "17 Days," and "She's Always In My Hair" attest to songs that stood on their own as first-rate soulful jams not just B-side placeholders.

For example, "Erotic City," a sleazy groove sex funk jam, is on the B-sides of the 7- and 12-inch vinyl singles of "Let's Go Crazy," with its rock virtuoso solo guitar-laden riffs. "Erotic City" was a B-side ode to sex that had Prince and Sheila E. (Sheila Escovedo) singing a kinky duet about how they "fuck so pretty." Moreover, "Erotic City" was no one-off but more like a bonus cut from Sheila E.'s *The Glamorous Life* (1984), a six-track percussion-driven solo LP release. With *The Glamorous Life*, as was the case with The Time, Prince was in deep disguise, writing, playing, and producing R&B-oriented music for another artist.

Once again, Prince wrote and recorded some of the most interesting and original music operating under the veneer of "The Starr Company," and allocating writing credit for all the songs to the featured artist on the release (Sheila E.). As a result, Sheila E.'s prodigious percussion took center stage as a performer. In this case, the lead song and title of the album, "The Glamorous Life," became the breakout single, a daring mix of propulsive afro-Cuban percussion, sax solos, and new wave chords. The Prince track shot up to #1 on the *Billboard* Dance Club chart and made it to #7 on the *Billboard* Hot 100 list. With the "The Glamorous Life" Prince created a more organic sounding electro-dance version of the Latin freestyle sound found on Shannon's groundbreaking monster dance-floor hit "Let the Music Play" (1983). Granted, *Glamorous Life* preceded the *Purple Rain* LP by a few weeks but it foretold a more accurate musical bearing for where Prince was headed in the future than *Around the World in a Day*. *Glamorous Life* tracks like the discordant funk instrumental "Shortberry Strawcake" prefigured Prince's next proxy project, *The Family* (1985), a studio release that dropped only four months after the release of *ATWD* and was another music project rooted in R&B.

Prince was the author and musician on the self-titled LP, *The Family* and, as on the first Time album, Prince's vocals are discernible; it almost makes *The Family* a Prince solo album in all but appearance. The material was a horn-centric, sax-heavy, pop-funk-filled album full of jazzy arrangements. Tracks such as "Yes," "High Fashion," and "Susannah's Pajamas" are notable jams that featured dynamic sax solos minus the phrasing clichés that often accompany pop garden-variety sax solos. The breakout single, "The Screams of Passion," also avoided R&B platitudes by incorporating cerebral string arrangements and a discordant rhythmic melody. As a consequence, "The Screams of Passion" sounded like an experimental version of Barry White's midtempo symphonic dance music, a style most associated with White's Love Unlimited Orchestra. Although the lead performers of the group were a white woman, Susannah Melvoin, and a white man, Paul Peterson, "The Screams of Passion" climbed to #9 on the *Billboard* Black Music Chart.

Despite a well-conceived and executed musical effort the look of the group was unconvincing. The album cover displayed a headshot of Susannah and Paul huddled together and staring in opposite directions. Despite their intimate proximity to one another the duo looked like two estranged members from the Mickey Mouse Club, dressed in drag, and forced to pretend they liked each other. There was some truth to the glaring artifice represented on the album cover. Susannah was romantically involved with Prince, which possibly accounts for the emotionally detached expressions the pair conveyed on the album cover.

The only two black members of The Family seemed equally out of place as the lead members. Jellybean Jonson was the drummer and Jerome Benton reprised his role as the consummate utility performer as a dancer and faux conductor for the music video version of "The Screams of Passion." Adding even more visual dissonance to the video was showing Eric Leeds, a proven reedman that delivered the dazzling saxophone overdubs on the album, playing the bass guitar. Most likely, *The Family* album would have remained relegated to obscurity if it were not for Sinéad O'Connor remaking a little-known ballad from the album five years later. The Prince-penned "Nothing Compares 2 U" became an international pop hit when Sinéad remade the track on her sophomore album *I Do Not Want What I Haven't Got* (1990) and starred in a haunting video of the song.

For a majority of fans Prince's *Purple Rain* was the apex of his creative success and *ATWD* a testament to his maverick vision. For his detractors,

Purple Rain and *ATWD* are examples of Prince catering to crossover ambitions. But for those willing to follow Prince off the beaten path there were a multitude of sonic surprises that continually eschewed the pop-rock material and rock status he cultivated with *Purple Rain*. Ultimately, Prince's "hiding in plain sight" shenanigans succeeded in obscuring his involvement with various R&B experimental groups. Nonetheless, these side music projects demonstrated how black music idioms of funk and, to a lesser extent, jazz were the primary styles Prince continually used to work out ideas and perfect his sound. In particular, Prince introduced horns into his music with *The Glamorous Life* and *The Family*, but even the truncated *Purple Rain* tour was a harbinger of Prince moving toward more horn-filled soul and funk arrangements.

Although the *Purple Rain* tour showcased Prince's most signature band configuration of The Revolution, whereby Wendy and Lisa had established themselves as prominent figures, a counter-prevailing force was gaining momentum as the concert tour drew to a close. The last leg of the tour heralded the addition of Eric Leeds to the concerts for extended saxophone solos that later usurped Wendy's guitar solo on "Purple Rain."[27] Prince's inclusion of a horn section on the tour further signaled a growing impatience with the pop constraints of *Purple Rain*. Musicologist Griffin Woods makes a key observation concerning the inescapable black racial connotation of Prince introducing horns into his music: "Prince made his name in the early 1980s as a stylistic provocateur whose blend of rock guitar and new wave synthesizers pushed the cutting edge of pop music in 1982 with *1999* and again in 1984 with *Purple Rain*. In his earlier career, Prince had avoided using horns entirely to distinguish himself from older styles of black music."[28]

By encouraging Leeds to take the stage for lengthy sax solos, Leeds effectively brings the black musical idioms of jazz and funk music to the foreground in Prince's music. Sure Wendy and Lisa flanked Prince at various awards shows, shared the cover of *Rolling Stone* magazine with him, and are fabled Prince musical conspirators. But Leeds was a central and indispensable sonic force during Prince's post–*Purple Rain* creative peak over several years and various projects.

As discrete events the release of *The Glamorous Life*, shifting horn arrangements on the *Purple Rain* tour, and the release of the saxophone-heavy *The Family* LP appear obscure and uncalculated. Taken as a whole (and including a couple decades of hindsight), the inclusion of "horns" signposts how Prince's musical palette was more complicated than the "white" cock-rocker aesthetic used to punctuate the conclusion of *Purple Rain* or the anemic impression of a rock-auteur advanced with the release of *Around the World in a Day*. On the one hand, Prince incorporated signature sonic elements associated with African American music genres on side projects and B-side material to enhance the sonic tapestry of his own music. On the other hand, with his *Family* side project whiteness is placed center stage. Perhaps this tactic of privileging whiteness was a relic from Prince trying to circumvent the racial politics of MTV programming that demanded a diminished black presence. Admittedly, the reason(s) for continuing tactics that obscured and hid Prince's black music sensibility are up for debate but the result was quite conclusive. For all of Prince's personal drive and racial hide-and-seek, for good and for bad, the strictures of American popular culture marked the racial parameters his career confronted and accommodated during the mid-1980s. And Prince, at least for a moment, redefined the scope of pop music to include blackness as a dominant presence.

Even Rick James, his most vocal critic and adversary, capitulated to the power and popularity of *Purple Rain* to circumvent the strident racial challenges of the music industry and achieve crossover success. In the recent past, James called Prince a creep and racial sellout.[29] But on the heels of *Purple Rain* James gave his best Prince imitation in a music video for the lead single off James's studio LP *Glow* (1985). The music video ostensibly has James reprising Prince's role as The Kid and, like in *Purple Rain*, the music video for "Glow" uses the backstage setting of the dressing room as a prominent site of discussion and reflection. The video begins with James in his dressing room dressed in an Edwardian lace white billowing blouse, his hair dyed blonde, and lamenting his life as a self-destructive musician, a prevalent theme throughout *Purple Rain*. Later, James is on stage wearing a trench coat, begins playing an all-white electric guitar, and delivers a rousing performance in front of a racially mixed audience. Look and sound familiar? Even for his rivals, the Prince crossover formula appeared to offer the best opportunity to grasp boundary-defying commercial success.

As Prince moved into the 1990s the crossover approach would increasingly sour as a source of mainstream appeal. Instead, a new, urgent, and racially assertive form of music was gaining ground as a cultural and economic force in the American recording industry and American pop culture—hip-hop. In 1983 Charlie Ahern's film *Wild Style* forewarned of the monumental shift in black music and popular culture on the horizon. Remarkably, the film is quite similar to *Purple Rain* in form. *Wild Style* presented a motley crew of endearing nonprofessional thespians, playing themselves, in a loosely scripted narrative that relied heavily on musical performances and culminated with a series of musical acts on stage. But the two films diverged in content and ideological implication. *Purple Rain* situated a white rock crossover sensibility as a central quality and goal. *Wild Style*, like the environment hip-hop emerged from, presented, and stayed with, a stark urban street aesthetic filled with black and brown characters struggling under a decaying social infrastructure.

Wild Style, unlike *Purple Rain*, fell flat at the box office. The film, however, would carve out a niche as a cult classic and stand as a significant cultural artifact for chronicling the birth of hip-hop before the genre emerged as a dominant cultural force a decade later. For Prince, hip-hop was more than a radical break in form and content from prior musical styles. Hip-hop resurrected impulses and anxieties presumed exhausted with the disappearance of blaxploitation cinema in the late 1970s. Most important, for Prince as a crossover, androgynous, and ersatz biracial pop figure, hip-hop proved a vexing challenge for him to engage issues concerning black militancy, hyperblack masculinity, and black racial authenticity on hip-hop's own aesthetic and ideological terms. Interestingly, in his next film Prince confronted several of these racial anxieties playing, of all things, a racially aware, belligerent, and seemingly bisexual black man in *Under The Cherry Moon* (1986).

4

Cherry Bomb

---

*He plays guitar and piano and plays
them very well. But it's the church thing
that I hear in his music that makes him
special, and that organ thing. It's a black
thing and not a white thing . . .*
—Miles Davis, *Miles: The
Autobiography*

For *Purple Rain* moviegoers that did not leave their seats until the theater
lights came on (I was one of many), at the conclusion of the credits for the
film the phrase "May u live 2 see the dawn" scrolled up the screen. At best,
the phrase was a cryptic quasi-religious tagline, but for wishful fans like
myself, the words signaled the title for the *Purple Rain* sequel—*The Dawn*.
Given how the actual follow-up film to *Purple Rain* baffled moviegoers and
film critics alike, a more fitting title for Prince's sophomore film would have
been *The Setting*. In reality, the name of Prince's next film was *Under the
Cherry Moon* (1986), a bona fide box-office bomb. Only the music from the
motion picture was exceptional, a bohemian funk stew full of blaring horns,
flute chirps, staccato rhythms, saxophone licks, acoustic instrumentation,
a fledgling rap flow, sleazy accordion riffs, and multi-overdubbed voices. A

driving dance beat rested at the center of the chaotic soundscape, which was periodically accented with Al Green–like soulful falsetto phrasings. The LP was Prince's eighth studio release and was entitled *Parade: Music from the Motion Picture Under the Cherry Moon* (1986). In comparison to the *ATWD* release *Parade* was a revitalized and fresh sound.

Parade dropped three months before the release of *Under the Cherry Moon*, and the positive critical reception of the album made the prospect of the film seem all the more promising. The LP's subtitle, *Music from the Motion Picture Under the Cherry Moon*, situated *Parade* as a sonic promo of the film, and the images outside and inside the album cover functioned as a static prescreening of Prince's upcoming motion picture. The cover of the LP saw Prince ditch the colorful purple trench coat, lace ruffled shirts, and curly top bouffant hairdo. In its place was a black and white picture of an ultra-sleek Prince sporting a low-key pompadour; a black, skintight midriff shirt; black, low-waisted hip-hugging pants; and black high-heeled boots. Inside the LP cover various images of Prince and The Revolution appeared like movie stills from the film. One picture even showed Prince wearing a tuxedo and sporting a finger-wave hairstyle accented with a part.

The promotional music videos for the *Parade* release were just as distinctive as the images on and inside the jacket LP. For the "Mountains" music video Prince wore an oversized black caballero hat and black bolero crop top. The synthesis of all these new elements was on full display on the austere, yet visually captivating, music video "Kiss," a breakout hit single from the *Parade* release. For the "Kiss" video Prince wore a svelte version of black palazzo pants paired with a black crop top, but for a significant portion of his performance he was simply shirtless. The new romantic Prince persona of the past was stylishly updated and replaced by a fashionably innovative Prince who was no longer content with adopting emergent fashion trends. Instead, he was creating his own, more independent, fashion forward and sophisticated look.

If *Under the Cherry Moon* proved successful it would dispel doubts that *Purple Rain* was a fluke and prove Prince was a true box office draw and authentic leading man. If accurate then Prince would join the ranks of standout mega music stars that achieved cinematic success as leading men like Frank Sinatra, Elvis Presley, and, to a lesser extent, David Bowie and Sting. To facilitate Prince's leading man perception MTV and Warner Bros. Pictures decided to use a promotional contest to launch *Under the Cherry Moon*. In the old Hollywood studio system of yesteryear, fan-centered

publicity stunts helped confer and confirm the matinee idol status for leading men and women actors.[1] Moreover and most often, such PR events were
pre-scripted and staged.[2] Interestingly, MTV and Warner Bros. Pictures
decided to leave their PR stunt entirely to chance and sponsored a call-in
contest whereby the ten thousandth caller won hosting privileges for the premier of *Under the Cherry Moon*. Lisa Barber, a twenty-year-old white
woman, won a movie date with Prince, and her small hometown of Sheridan, Wyoming, a population of 10,369, would host a big-time movie
premier.

It almost goes without saying, a culturally conservative High Plains ham-
let and a state that claims former Vice President Richard Cheney as one of
Wyoming's favorite sons is not the most auspicious setting for debuting a
film about two black men living in France conning rich middle-aged white
women out of their money for sexual favors.[3] Most likely, a more favorable
fit for the folks of Sheridan was the "heartland rock" of John Cougar
Mellencamp or having a musician like Willie Nelson visit. At the time,
Nelson had just finished spearheading the first Farm Aid benefit concert to
help save family farms from foreclosure. Prince, acting as a cabaret gigolo,
was a tough sell in a white small town like Sheridan. Moreover, the music
for the film was a long way away from the rock riffs that permeated the
Purple Rain soundtrack. In contrast, the music from *Parade* was where
Prince chose "to play up the black side of his multifaceted musical sensibility."[4] Given the remote setting of the film's premiere, it is easy to declare
Under the Cherry Moon suffered from a marketing blunder. Nevertheless,
if Prince was going to achieve crossover leading man status the film would
have to, as the saying goes, "play in Peoria," then Sheridan, Wyoming, would
truly test Prince's crossover leading man appeal. The film received a lukewarm response from the Sheridan audience.[5]

Under the Cherry Moon did not fare any better after a national release.
The film was widely panned by critics and, at best, barely grossed ten million dollars or barely broke even. In reality, it might have come up a few million short.[6] Only the most fervent fans would advocate the merits of the
film as good entertainment. Ostensibly, the film contained all the ingredi-
ents that made *Purple Rain* a hit, Prince and music by Prince. The film even
included Jerome Benton reprising, more or less, his standout sideman comic
routine with Prince instead of Morris Day. Despite such similarities to
Purple Rain they were not enough to overcome a variety of weaknesses present in *Under the Cherry Moon*. What happened to make *Under the*

Cherry Moon bomb at the box office? First and foremost, the film was hampered by the hubris of its star. Early in the shooting Prince usurped the director's chair from Mary Lambert over "creative differences." Not surprisingly, because of the severely inadequate directorial skills of Prince, the film was a hot mess.

Under the direction of Albert Magnoli, in *Purple Rain*, Prince showed flashes of brilliance with his uneven rendition of a tortured artist and when acting opposite Clarence Williams III, as the sensitive son to the latter's domineering father. In addition, another well-acted segment in *Purple Rain* is Prince's posttraumatic suicide scene and stands as his most challenging and successful dramatic part. In *Under the Cherry Moon*, as his own director, Prince was melodramatic and constantly mugged to the camera, as if in a constant state of sexual arousal. If this was the point, then Prince successfully provided plenty of optic foreplay. Prince appeared more concerned with wooing his viewing audience than any love interest in the film, with his sultry glances, fingertip licking, affected mannerisms, and prolonged eye contact into the camera. There are no standout dramatic moments in *Under the Cherry Moon*. The film oscillates between camp and kitsch. To add insult to injury, Prince and his female co-star, Kristen Scott Thomas, were devoid of any sexual, romantic, or even platonic chemistry. Like a porcupine at a petting zoo, their on-screen pairing looked at odds and frequently painful.

Second, the music from the *Parade* album, the strongest feature of the film, was often barely audible and played in the background of various scenes. In *Purple Rain* the music was the star "character," and the captivating performances mitigated a threadbare narrative, stilted dialogue, and the limited acting chops of the cast. *Purple Rain* provided twelve musical performances. Surprisingly, *Under the Cherry Moon* delivered two, and one of them was absent Prince. Last, but not least, *Under the Cherry Moon* was presented in black and white cinematography, a choice that was alienating to the audience and contributed to the film earning critical derision and popular indifference.[7] As a consequence, *Under the Cherry Moon* easily courts consideration as a vapid, self-indulgent vanity film and an underwhelming follow-up to the dynamic *Purple Rain*. Despite these manifest shortcomings there is an aesthetic sumptuousness to the film found in virtually every scene. Moreover, in my mind, the problem with *Under the Cherry Moon* concerns categorization more than content and audience expectation more than directorial execution.

Without a doubt, *Under the Cherry Moon* is a woeful contender as a mainstream major motion picture but as an experimental "art house" film, *Under the Cherry Moon* is more accomplished. The art house quality of *Under the Cherry Moon* is immediately witnessed in Michael Ballhaus's efforts as the cinematographer for *Under the Cherry Moon*. His cinematography clearly imbued the film with technical maturity and optic elegance, a quality accredited to Ballhaus as the acclaimed film cinematographer on Martin Scorsese's *The Color of Money* (1986), *The Last Temptation of Christ* (1988), *Goodfellas* (1990), *The Age of Innocence* (1993), *Gangs of New York* (2002), and *The Departed* (2006), and Francis Ford Coppola's *Dracula* (1992). *Under the Cherry Moon* also invokes the stylistic film cues of Italian neorealism with its black and white cinematography, a preference for location filming, the recurrent presence of children, the use of nonprofessional actors, and a narrative focus on the poor and lower working class.[8] The sum of these stylistic cues makes *Under the Cherry Moon* a film more akin to a Federico Fellini–inspired art film than a retread of madcap Hollywood films from the 1940s, an aesthetic comparison used to criticize and occasionally praise *Under the Cherry Moon* for mimicking.[9]

As an art house film, *Under the Cherry Moon* would have had more leeway to rein in expectations that the film was geared toward mainstream appeal and commercial profit. Arguably, the film would have benefited from a big city premiere in New York or Los Angeles. Both New York and Los Angeles have vibrant antiestablishment art communities, which the film could have courted and used to blunt sharp criticism that the film was a commercial flop and lacked mainstream appeal. Perhaps none of these elements would have negated the shortcomings of *Under the Cherry Moon* if the film were more accurately viewed as an art film. Simply stated, *Under the Cherry Moon* could have just as likely invited criticism as an art house flop. Either way, as a moribund version of mainstream musical film duds like *Xanadu* (1980), a roller disco fantasy flick with its B-movie special effects, or a cloying attempt at artistic prestige, *Under the Cherry Moon* was a flop. Nevertheless the film was chockfull of subversive statements about race. To this point, *Under the Cherry Moon* is most noteworthy for critiquing white privilege, asserting the creative power of black culture, and rejecting the race-neutral positionality of *Purple Rain*'s character The Kid.

The setting for *Under the Cherry Moon* is Nice, France. Admittedly, the Old World opulence and aristocratic atmosphere of a European coastal city are far from the American shore and stateside racial politics. Nonetheless,

All three principal characters, Christopher Tracy (Prince), Tricky (Jerome Benton), and Mary (Kristen Scott Thomas), *Under the Cherry Moon* (1986)

given France's historical status as a refuge for African American intellectuals and musicians the French location signifies a deeper relevance and relationship to American racial politics than surface appearances. Legendary stage performer Josephine Baker; literary luminaries Richard Wright, Chester Himes, Langston Hughes, and James Baldwin; along with jazz giants Miles Davis, Lester Gordon, Bud Powell, Kenny Clarke, Nina Simone, and pioneering film maker Melvin Van Peebles all spent considerable time in France and, relative to America, extolled the racially liberating experience of living there.[10] *Under the Cherry Moon* draws on this past with a narrative concerning two African American men, Christopher (Prince) and Tricky (Jerome Benton), living in France as sex workers. Admittedly, Christopher and Tricky act more like juvenile goofballs than political expatriates. They frolic around France as bankrupt black gigolos dedicated to providing sexual services to wealthy white women and bilking them for as much money as possible. Nevertheless, the pair signifies numerous black Americans who chose to consciously relocate from America to France or live in Europe as an act of racial resistance.[11]

Presumably, *Under the Cherry Moon* is about Christopher conning Mary (Kristen Scott Thomas), a white heiress due to receive her $50 million trust fund when she turns twenty-one, out of her money. That was the plan, until Christopher falls in love with his mark and turns out to be a gigolo with a heart of gold. From a conventional Hollywood film perspective, *Under the*

Cherry Moon is a sugarcoated morality tale about the power of love to transcend money and social stature. On an ideological level, the film is much more subversive in its critique of broader race relations, racial assumptions, and cultural antagonism circulating in the film and, by extension, white society. The film uses Christopher and, to a lesser extent, Tricky as figures of sexual dread and delight to criticize and bring into sharp relief a variety of binary oppositions throughout the film; such as black versus white, poor versus rich, and male versus female. For example, early in the film, a birthday party scene conveys how Christopher and Tricky embody the pleasure promised by the black body in contrast to the requirements, responsibilities, and surefooted expectations of white privilege.

Mary's exclusive twenty-first birthday party is set at her father's grand estate, a picturesque cliffside chateau overlooking the sea where butlers, maids, high-fashion friends, and sophisticated associates mill about with an air of detached decorum until Mary makes her grand entrance. Mary enters the courtyard and opens a full-body towel to reveal her nude body, then boasts that her "birthday suit" is an original design. Her immodest display of nudity and radical disruption of the subdued formality of the event are meant to signal her outlaw orientation, a character trait fully affirmed when she later proceeds to commandeer the nearby bandstand. She pushes the drummer off his seat and take his place to perform a drum riff while chanting, "Planet rock / you just don't stop." The lyrics are lifted from the rap song "Planet Rock" (1982), an electro-funk hip-hop anthem. Mary uses rhythm and rap to reinforce her rebel credentials and signal how black expressive culture is a disruptive presence and cultural affront to the frigid white haute bourgeois sensibility on prominent display.

Mary's paltry rap performance also telegraphs she is superficially familiar with blackness but also enthralled with the possibility of exploring how blackness is a meaningful source of identity, human expression, and rebellion. Most importantly, the disruptive anxieties around sex, signaled by her exhibitionistic nudity and race, vis-à-vis hip-hop music, are merged, amplified, and embodied by Christopher and Tricky when they crash Mary's birthday party as uninvited guests. Against a backdrop of overwhelming economic affluence and a white racial setting, Christopher and Tricky, as symbols of real and imagined sexual incursion, constantly poke, prod, and peel away at Mary's white privileged position. For instance, Mary's friends browbeat her to answer a call from her family-approved boyfriend after Tricky easily coaxes her to join in leading a conga line. Later, white medi-

Prince's optic foreplay in *Under the Cherry Moon* (1986)

ocrity is critiqued when Christopher surreptitiously overhears Mary listening to her boyfriend serenade her over the phone by singing "Happy Birthday to You." Christopher snidely remarks, her boyfriend is no Billy Eckstine, a swing-era African American crooner known for his smooth vocal delivery.

Mary's conga line participation and badgered departure establishes the tensions between the black body as a source of adventurism, emotionality, immediacy, and pleasure against the drab requirements, responsibilities, and expectations of white privilege. Moreover, Christopher's snide remark about the quality of her boyfriend's singing highlights the implicit critique of whiteness churning just below the surface of such scenes and signifies the racial fault lines present throughout the film. Throughout the remainder of the film self-congratulatory racial blackness is used to undermine and attack white privilege with racial barbs, subtle semiotics, and overt symbolism to critique whiteness as decadent, patently false, absurd, and droll.

For example, the centrality and value of blackness over racial whiteness is asserted when Mary makes a surprise visit to Christopher's apartment and sees him wearing a "doo-rag" around his head. Mary dismissively flicks his forehead and asks in a repulsed manner, "What is this?" Christopher proudly retorts, "Soul!" Strictly speaking, do-rags are silk headscarves often wrapped

Signifying defiant black cool with an album cover of Miles Davis, *Under the Cherry Moon* (1986)

around the back of the head and tied at the front of the head into a knot. African American men frequently use a version of the do-rag to not only hold chemically processed hairstyles in place while sleeping but braided and "wave" hairstyles too. In *Under the Cherry Moon*, Christopher's do-rag functions as a powerful signifier of racial difference, insurgency, pride, and politics vis-à-vis the term "soul," an expression and sensibility that came to prominence during the Black Power movement of the late 1960s.[12] But without a doubt, the clearest and best racially subversive rebuke of the privileged place whiteness has in the film is when Christopher goads Mary into repeatedly reading aloud the words "wreka stow" written on a napkin.

With her highbrow English accent and literal vocal articulation of the phrase the cultural dissonance between whiteness and blackness is brought into its starkest relief. After each repetition Christopher and Tricky display increasing degrees of raucous laughter to the visible disdain of white patrons dining at the lavish restaurant. Accordingly, Mary's frustration intensifies from their refusal to tell her the meaning of the words and what is funny about saying them. Eventually, Christopher helps her decode her repeated utterances by asking her, "If you wanted to buy a Sam Cooke album, where would you go?" Mary answers, "the wreka stow" (read record store). Not all racial critiques were as well executed as the "wreka stow" vignette in establishing the centrality and value of blackness over the insults and demeaning status it occupies in the white world presented in the film.

A regressive racial theme surfaces when Christopher chastises Mary about how she feels after kissing a black man and ponders how she will react when she has intercourse with one.

CHRISTOPHER: It's different than it is with your rich boyfriend.

MARY: It's not so hot; you bit me and your hair is greasy!

CHRISTOPHER: "Christopher this is nice, I've never done it on a piano before."

MARY: Oh, you're obnoxious!

CHRISTOPHER: You're probably quiet at first. "Oh, oh." Then you get loud. "Oh! Oh!" And then *you get black*. [emphasis mine] "Oh, shit! Christopher, oh shit! Oh, baby, oh no!"

At its most retrograde, Christopher's and Mary's antagonisms and sexual assumptions appear plagiarized from American cinema's racist past of portraying hypersexualized black bucks waylaying white women with their powerful genitals, an archetype immortalized with the blackface performance of Gus (Walter Long) as a black rapist in *Birth of a Nation* (1915). This type of black representation stoked sexual paranoia and justified decades of black men being lynched.

At its most progressive, Christopher's commentary evokes the antihero character of Sweetback from Melvin Van Peeble's seminal blaxploitation film *Sweet Sweetback's Badasssss Song* (1971), a film about an African American male sex worker that performs various sex acts on his odyssey from unaware criminal to conscious black militant. Arguably, the radical sexual statement of *Sweet Sweetback's Badasssss Song* became the predominant mode for imagining black male sexuality in blaxploitation cinema during the 1970s. In particular, blaxploitation used the black pimp as a type of urban folk antihero archetype, a representational trope present in films such as *Trick Baby* (1972), *The Mack* (1973), *Truck Turner* (1974), *Willie Dynamite* (1974), and *Dolemite* (1975). Even though *Under the Cherry Moon* reanimated tropes of black male sexuality as a dangerous presence and source of transgression for white women, the film blatantly challenged well-worn aesthetic cues and emotional assumptions concerning black masculinity in American cinema.

First, *Under the Cherry Moon* clearly stakes out an unprecedented portrayal of black masculinity in American film by having Prince play a gigolo in his film. Certainly, a variety of white characters have occupied the role of a gigolo in American films. Arguably, the most notable examples are the critically acclaimed *Midnight Cowboy* (1969) and the vexing *American Gigolo* (1980). The former is about an idealistic male hustler and his down-and-out friend scraping by in New York City. The latter presents a film about a swank male-hustler living in Los Angeles. An interesting point of analysis, for both films, is how the figure of the male prostitute is constructed as a bisexual figure. In *Midnight Cowboy*, the childhood trauma of Joe Buck (Jon Voight) is a catalyst for his adult homosexual encounters. In *American Gigolo*, Julian (Richard Gere) pleads to turn tricks for Leon's (Bill Duke) homosexual clients and train new male recruits to do the same if Leon ceases framing him for a sadomasochistic sex murder he did not commit. In both films, a bisexual orientation surfaces as points of trauma and duress. In contrast, *Under the Cherry Moon* signals a homoerotic sensibility as a point of playfulness and an expression of honest emotional intercourse, a sensibility strongly telegraphed by Prince's character. In this sense, Prince presented a black character at odds with the black buck and black macho poses respectively found in Hollywood movies of the past and throughout blaxploitation cinema.

Perhaps as media scholar Lisa Taylor declared, Prince was too diminutive in stature "to ever qualify as a dominant conventional macho male; indeed his physicality places him on rather more equal terms with women. More at home as the 'switch,' he occupied a number of sexual subjectivities, often moving between dominant and submissive roles at will, demonstrating the non-fixity of heterosexuality."[13] In this manner, Prince faced a formidable aesthetic challenge with his small, lithe, pubescent, girl-like build relative to blaxploitation cinema actors, such as Fred Williamson, Jim Brown, Richard Roundtree, Ron O'Neal, and Jim Kelly, that showcased their athletic physiques to signify their supermacho attitude and sexual appeal. In comparison to Hollywood films prior to blaxploitation cinema, representations of black male sexuality had a history of presenting black men, for the most part, as neutered asexual characters, a figure repeatedly embodied in the roles that Sidney Poitier played in the 1950s and 1960s.[14]

The anti-macho posture of Prince's version of a black gigolo hints at the bisexuality of both characters in *Under the Cherry Moon* and suggests Christopher's heterosexual choices are driven by economic crisis. Presumably, the film constructs Christopher as competing against Tricky for Mary's

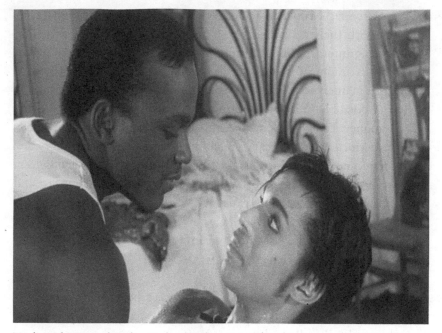

Tricky and Prince take a dip, *Under the Cherry Moon* (1986)

affection. But there is a persistent dissonance throughout the film concerning the heterosexual chemistry between Christopher and Mary. On the whole, Christopher and Mary's attraction to one another is dull, feeble, mechanical, and unconvincing. Arguably, the most compelling sexual spark exists between Christopher and Tricky. Several scenes in the film affirm a romantic homoerotic undertone to the nature, tension, and quality of their relationship. For instance, the homoerotic tenor of their relationship is established early in the film when Christopher is shown taking a bath and playing with a rubber duck as Tricky tosses flower petals into the water while they discuss current events. Certainly, as roommates, a degree of close social proximity is warranted, but the film persists in showing the two men in ways that go beyond spatial closeness and connote sexual intimacy. For example, after Christopher slips exiting the bathtub Tricky catches him. They embrace in a lovers' clench, frozen in a face-to-face cuddle, staring deeply into one another's eyes for a prolonged interval before Tricky releases his clasp and Christopher slips to the floor.

Despite their overt claims concerning their heterosexual "player" status the most genuine and enduring expression of intimacy in *Under the Cherry*

Moon is between the two men, a point signaled early in the film when Tricky is shown with the female manager of their apartment complex, behind a check-in counter, engaging in an impromptu make-out session. Just as their intimate moment is on the verge of increasing its intensity Christopher barges in unexpectedly, and the young white woman scrambles to close her unbuttoned blouse before berating Christopher and Tricky for owing her rent money. Tricky is also repeatedly shown engaging in a clichéd form of queer performance that relies on flamboyant visual and auditory cues, such as feminine mannerisms and adopting a feminine voice when onscreen. Such symbolic conceits suggest that something is not what it appears and that both men are engaging in sexual activity with white women for cash but are really interested in each other as lovers, a point underscored when Christopher ponders the existential meaning of life while he and Tricky take a walk through the city.

> CHRISTOPHER: If two people really dug one another they couldn't be torn apart no matter what. For example—do you love me? C'mon Tricky, you know what I'm talking about.
> TRICKY: Girl, I loved you for years.
> CHRISTOPHER: Tricky. Seriously. Do you?
> TRICKY: Well, yeah. I guess.
> CHRISTOPHER: Yes?
> TRICKY: Yeah! Yeah!

This declaration of devotion is later sealed with a kiss after Christopher places a necktie around Tricky, touches two fingers to his mouth, and tenderly touches Tricky on his cheek before leaving.

In addition to the nearly incessant display of both men staring into each other's eyes (as if they are about to kiss), a pivotal scene reveals the emotional stakes between the two after Christopher reneges on a prearranged dinner date with Tricky to surreptitiously meet with Mary instead.

> TRICKY: "I'll meet you at the club in two hours."
> CHRISTOPHER: I got waylaid.
> TRICKY: No, you got laid. You dogged me. You lied to me! You broke the rules of our partnership. You're jive and you got laid.
> CHRISTOPHER: Tricky. You're cute, but you're not my wife.
> TRICKY: Why you selfish son of a biscuit eater. I thought we were partners.

The flat chemistry between Prince and Kristen on display, *Under the Cherry Moon* (1986)

A portion of their row continues with Christopher lying in bed and Tricky sitting next to him, signaling their confrontation is less of a business rift and more of a lover's quarrel. As far as Tricky is concerned, detached intercourse with rich white women is condoned, but having a sincere emotional bond with a white client is a betrayal to their authentic and sincere companionship.

Arguably, as black bisexual gigolos, both characters occupied a relatively original space in black cinema and made *Under the Cherry Moon* a precursor to and prototype for more independent movies that explored the sexual politics of desire and homoerotic friendships in such films as *My Own Private Idaho* (1991), *Y Tu Mamá También* (2001), and *Moonlight* (2016). Admittedly, these three films are well acted and accomplished in contrast to *Under the Cherry Moon*, a film that reeks of self-indulgence and amateur acting. But in terms of an impressionistic cultural statement, *Under the Cherry Moon* offers a prescient example of a burgeoning aesthetic associated with sexually deconstructing the mainstream Hollywood buddy film genre, a la *Brokeback Mountain* (2006), along with challenging longstanding strident notions of black masculinity amplified by blaxploitation cinema and, later, in the late 1990s, when hip-hop excavated the decrepit bones of

Tricky and Prince's sexual tension is so thick you can almost cut it with a knife, *Under the Cherry Moon* (1986).

blaxploitation pimp iconography and reanimated an even more exaggerated typology of black hypermasculinity.

Ideologically, *Under the Cherry Moon*, with its interracial desires and homoerotic impulses, was a symbolic affront to the New Right politics of the Reagan era that promoted a return and reaffirmation of traditional family values and heterosexual piety, a position that fueled a policy of indifference to the mounting AIDS (acquired immunodeficiency syndrome) crisis of the 1980s.[15] In terms of entertainment value, *Under the Cherry Moon* provided what fandom values most—to see and know the objects of their adoration as they actually are. As counterintuitive as it first appears, the ill-conceived decision to allow Prince to direct *Under the Cherry Moon* provided a more sustained glimpse of Prince Rogers Nelson the person, rather than Prince the performer.

Under the Cherry Moon dispensed with what Prince did best in *all* his films—perform music. Instead, *Under the Cherry Moon* encompassed what Prince did worst on celluloid—act. As a result, Prince is unable to convincingly embody his character, a black gigolo from Miami stuck in the South of France "tryin' to make a dollar out of fifteen cents." Rather, the character of Christopher Tracy is more reflective of a jubilant and smug black musician from Minnesota, interacting with one of his band buddies and reenacting what they have already done. This point is underscored in the film with the "wrecka stow" scene, which is unadulterated Prince. The film exchange was a prominent staple of previous "inside" conversations and jokes with other musicians.[16] *Under the Cherry Moon* signaled that Prince was a prankster prone to spouting bad poetry and playing mind games with friends and foes alike, a person that played coy, liked to laugh, and was ruthlessly self-serving. Accordingly, Prince's overall presence in *Under the Cherry Moon* contributes to "demystifying his stage persona through a performance that is relaxed and conversational.[17]

Additionally, unlike the racially ambiguous and sullen character of The Kid in *Purple Rain*, Prince projects a clearly identifiable black racial sensibility while playing the Christopher Tracy character with gleeful élan. Admittedly, *Under the Cherry Moon* did not completely destroy lingering notions that Prince was no longer distancing himself from racial blackness. A dream sequence in the film seemed to signal that Prince was still committed to running away from blackness when Christopher encounters an older black woman and retreats in horror when she utters his name. Moreover, the prominent placement of a white female at the visual center of the film, along with having two white women in the "Kiss" music video, seemed indicative of an overattachment to whiteness.

However, in real life, Prince's increasing embrace of blackness became increasingly visible when The Revolution lineup was extended to include a few former black bodyguards as backup dancers, a shift that troubled his white bandmates.[18] Prince's white band members were right to be worried. Wendy and Lisa, the most prominent white members of the band, were soon fired, signaling that Prince's days of being a new wave weirdo were rapidly winding down. Instead, Prince started embracing a more soulful, funky, and African American–centered form of visual and sonic expression with his next studio album and the accompanying concert film, both entitled *Sign o' the Times* (1987), his Madhouse side-music projects, and the cancellation of *The Black Album* (1987).

Given how *Under the Cherry Moon* failed to meet the high expectations set by *Purple Rain* one could reasonably assume Prince would take a break from movie making. Instead, he decided to make a third movie on the heels of the second, a concert film. Perhaps, at least, in the immediate wake of *Under the Cherry Moon*, Prince recognized acting was not his strong suit. In any event, *Sign o' the Times* stayed in Prince's comfort zone by showcasing his singing and showmanship. Nonetheless, a concert film is an ambitious project. By their nature, concert movies are a puzzling hybrid, a recorded film of a live music performance striving to capture the ephemeral immediacy of an event. In this regard, not many concert films are able to achieve the goal of successfully capturing a compelling music performance. Most often the notable concert films appear driven by a broader commentary on a cultural phenomenon more than a music performance.

Case in point, *Woodstock* (1970) is a quintessential concert film and does more than document legendary rock musicians performing at the peak of their popularity. The film functions as a defining cultural touchstone that chronicles the halcyon days of the late 1960s counterculture movement in America. Concert films of this ilk are like time capsules containing the look and sound of a bygone era, rather than being compelling examples of recorded performances that were as exciting on screen as they were live at the venue. On the other end of the spectrum, the Talking Heads' *Stop Making Sense* (1984) is a magnificent concert film and conveys the energy and visual spectacle of the group's live performance. In terms of black concert films *Soul to Soul* (1971) and *Wattstack* (1973) are two notable entries. Both films are a celebration of black racial pride and black cultural expression in the immediate wake of the Black Power movement of the late 1960s.

Soul to Soul presents footage of popular African American soul singers and jazz musicians performing in Accra, Ghana, for the country's annual celebration of independence from colonial rule. *Wattstack* is more provincial but just as political. The film documents a tribute benefit concert marking the Watts rebellion of 1965 and offers a peek into the waning black power politics and black cultural nationalism of the early 1970s. In this sense, *Soul to Soul* and *Wattstack* are more than concert films; like *Woodstock*, they are cultural touchstones. In this case, both concert films document and capture the tenor of the times surrounding black cultural agency and identity. But if any of the artistic reveries are accurate about the concert footage of Aretha Franklin performing *Amazing Grace* (1972), one of the greatest gospel albums ever recorded, then the Franklin footage is sure to stand as the preeminent black concert film of our time. Given that footage of the Queen of Soul performing at the Los Angeles New Temple Missionary Baptist Church has finally emerged from legal limbo, perhaps a whole host of folk will witness a masterpiece in the making and be blessed.[19] It also remains to be seen if more contemporary concert films, such as *Fade to Black* (2004) and *Dave Chappelle's Block Party* (2006), are regarded, in the future, as classic concert films. Until then, in my mind, Prince's *Sign o' the Times* (1987) ranks as the top-tiered black concert film of the contemporary moment.

Ironically, the impetus for the *Sign o' the Times* concert film was the faltering sales of the album.[20] After the *Parade* release Prince churned out another double album to mark the release of his ninth album, containing nearly eighty minutes of music and sixteen songs. Yet, as amazing and impressive a feat as *Sign o' the Times* was, given that one man made so much music, the double album was actually a pared-down version of the original triple album Prince first submitted to Warner Bros. Records.[21] Just imagine if the original triple album version had made it past the gatekeepers at Warner. Arguably, the LP, popularly referred to as *Crystal Ball*, would have gone down as Prince's grand magna opus. *Crystal Ball* might have courted consideration, alongside Stevie Wonder's *Songs in the Key of Life* (1976), as one of the greatest musical achievements of all time. Instead, *Crystal Ball* spawned much of the mythology that surrounds "the vault," a crypt of unreleased Prince music linked to the period leading up to and closely after the release of *Sign o' the Times*.

Even though the double album was less than a fan favorite, and less than what Prince originally conceived, to his critics *Sign o' the Times* stands as one of Prince's most accomplished artistic releases and achievements.[22] Given Prince's box office failure with *Under the Cherry Moon* and the lagging sales of the *Sign o' the Times* album it is a curious choice for Prince to generate a concert film as the album's visual analogue. Moreover, Prince's economic and cultural clout had significantly dwindled. Accordingly, Prince was forced to work outside the traditional Hollywood system for his concert film. Nonetheless, Prince nimbly sidestepped mainstream studios no longer willing to gamble on the concert film he had shot and "inked a deal with Cineplex Odeon Films, the distribution side of a fifteen hundred screen Toronto-based theater chain," to bypass Hollywood movie studios.[23] Despite the maverick spirit infused in the creation and distribution of *Sign o' the Times*, the concert film was originally intended to play as a standard concert movie with footage consisting of live recordings from the *Sign o' the Times* European tour. Because the sound quality and footage of the original live recordings from the tour were faulty the footage was reshot on a soundstage at Paisley Park Studios.

The reshot footage included decorative lighting, an of assortment of large, flashing neon signs, oversized props, and a series of vignettes depicting relationships gone wrong, crammed in between musical numbers and even lip-syncing. As a result, *Sign o' the Times* was less like a conventional concert film and more like a postmodern theatrical performance piece. What started out as an ambitious marketing project to bolster the lagging sales of the *Sign o' the Times* album became a daring cinematic achievement. The reshot footage captured Prince's knack for putting on a visually captivating performance along with a display of impressive musicianship. In addition, the concert film mixed multiple black music traditions in look, sound, and style, a creative maneuver that made *Sign o' the Times* the best and most sustained recorded representation of Prince at the peak of black expressivity and soulful articulation.

Starting with the optics of *Sign o' the Times*, Prince's band was at its blackest. In contrast to The Revolution, Prince's most noteworthy and predominantly white touring band, the *Sign o' the Times* concert film band is predominantly black. Out of the eleven band members only three are white; Matt Fink on the keyboard, Eric Leeds on the saxophone, and Matt Bliss on the trumpet. In addition, Prince abandoned his penchant for placing a white or racially ambiguous woman as his object of sexual attention. Instead, the film showcased Catherine "Cat" Glover, an African American dancer from Chicago, Illinois. Throughout the film Cat shakes and shimmies, bumps and grinds, and periodically performs contemporary urban dances of the period while her energetic go-go dancer routines perfectly complement Prince's agile dance moves. In this manner, *Sign o' the Times* incorporated and presented a key element of the black aesthetic; black performativity centered on choreographed dancing.[24]

In terms of sound, the gospel impulse, another cornerstone of the black aesthetic, is highlighted in the film.[25] For example, Prince invokes the "black church" on the track "Hot Thing" by adding an organ as accompanying instrumentation to the electro-funk synthesizer riff that begins the song. Later, Boni Boyer is showcased giving a gospel-styled vocal accompaniment on the song "Forever in My Life." African American classical music, popularly known as jazz, is the other black music genre frequently signposted in the film. Case in point, the band performs a cover version of Charlie "Yardbird" Parker's bluesy bebop jazz classic "Now's the Time" (1945). Each musician provided a powerhouse solo interpretation of the Parker tune. Later, Prince musically name checks Duke Ellington by calling out, "A-train" in the middle of playing "It's Gonna Be a Beautiful Night," a raucous party jam dance track. On Prince's cue the band starts playing the signature riff from Ellington's big band jazz standard "Take the 'A' Train." The solo improvisational performances not only demonstrated the superior musical chops required to play in Prince's band but Prince's musical appreciation and connection to jazz vocabularies.

Prince's infatuation with the jazz aesthetic was telegraphed several months prior to the release of the concert film when he began surreptitiously defacing his own pop edifice with his Madhouse music side-project *8* (1987), a jazz-fusion album. Maneca Lightner posed as a pinup girl on the album cover and functioned as the group's cover model. The cover model was a deliberate misdirection to distance Prince from the project, but in reality the music was Prince and reedman Eric Leeds providing an assortment of saxophone overdubs on a variety of instrumental pop jazz tracks. *8*, and later *16* (1987), invoked the fusion funk of Herbie Hancock's seminal *Head Hunters* (1973) album. For my taste "1" was the standout track on the *8* album. The track displayed the musical genius of Prince and the yeoman chops of Leeds on the sax. On "1" Prince exhibits an uncanny ability to play alongside and respond to multiple saxophone overdubs in such a synergistic manner he created an organic "live"-sounding recording. Ultimately, the fusion jazz-funk experiments Prince workshopped on the Madhouse side-projects made their way to Prince the musician proper on the *Sign o' the Times* concert film, where Prince openly declared his connectivity with the jazz idiom by incorporating bebop and straight-ahead jazz riffs, and of course, kicking it with Miles Dewey Davis.

The sonic fusion between Prince and jazz literally manifested when Prince and the iconoclastic jazz legend Miles Davis publicly played together. Prince and Miles were already members of a behind-closed-doors mutual admiration society, but their musical bromance went public when Davis joined Prince on stage for an extended version of "It's Gonna Be a Beautiful Night," at a New Year's Eve show in 1987. Their New Year's Eve performance is historic, given that their mercurial nature as musicians and their iconic stature are case studies in the ontological poetics of black expressive style. Each one alone changed the course of music two or three times (which is a conservative estimate). Their public pairing also conveyed a broader politics of meaning concerning race given Davis's strident criticism of whiteness: he was once quoted as saying that if he had only an hour left to live he would prefer to spend it slowly choking a white man to death.[26] Such impetuous statements secured Davis's stature as a lightning rod of controversy concerning race relations in America and made his proclamations about music, musicians, and racial authenticity a benchmark for reverence or contempt for those critiqued.[27] Just ask jazz genius Wynton Marsalis.[28] For Miles Davis, the Prince of Darkness, ensconced in unforgiveable blackness and a true musical don, to perform a trumpet solo on Prince's bandstand meant Davis was announcing to the music world that Prince was a made man. For others, like Stanley Crouch, an accomplished and habitually insightful jazz critic, seeing Davis following Prince around on stage dressed in a purple two-piece suit was no musical anointing. Rather Davis's actions stood as a debased example of Davis pandering for popularity.[29]

Either way, footage of the performance shows that neither musician was able to derive much cultural capital from the other. Davis did not bolster Prince's jazz status since Prince gave his best impression of James Brown by directing the band to come in and drop out around Davis's horn riffs. Prince did not appear to boost Davis's esteem as a mainstream musician. Davis's musical phrasing was bland and jumbled against the propulsive groove Prince had established for Davis to ride. Although their pairing promised synergy, for the most part, on stage at least, the pair seemed musically awkward. They reminded me of two heavyweight boxers in the beginning of a bout where the first rounds are wasted "feeling each other out." No matter, one thing is certain, with Davis on the stage Prince was a long way from aping the white rock and roll tropes found in *Purple Rain* and on the *Around the World in a Day* album. By hanging with the "Great Miles Davis" Prince overtly signaled that jazz was part and parcel of his new "black" sound.

"It's Gonna Be a Beautiful Night," was the go-to track for Prince to showcase his funk-jazz iteration of the Minneapolis sound. The track was used as the sonic platform for Prince and Davis's musical sparring session and in the concert film. Deep into the extended jam portion of the film version of the song the horn section breaks into a dissonant funk lick with a muted trumpet riding on top of the melody. Unbeknownst to the audience, the riff was from a track entitled, "Rock-hard in a Funky Place," off of Prince's tenth studio release—*The Black Album* (1987/1994).

The Black Album was on the verge of an official release in early December 1987, and, unexpectedly, Prince marshaled a successful last-ditch effort to quash the album. Roughly half-million units were officially destroyed. Some were surreptitiously reproduced, and a limited number of promotional copies gained circulation in Europe. As a consequence, *The Black Album* became one of the most prized bootlegged collections in American music history.[30] In fact, *The Black Album* garnered such a mythological status that Hanif Kureishi, an acclaimed playwright and novelist, wrote a novel with the same title as the bootlegged LP. Kureishi's novel, *The Black Album* (1995), is set in late-1980s London society and is a coming-of-age story about a Pakistani student torn between a conservative Muslim community and white British club culture. Not many, if any, musicians can claim their bootleg release was used as an ideological fulcrum to explore the sociopolitical polarities of postcolonial studies.[31] Given the frenzy for and elevated status of *The Black Album* in the wake of Prince shelving the release, it begs the question, Why was the album canceled in the first place?

The standard response to the foregoing question posits that Prince had second thoughts about releasing *The Black Album* because it was too negative.[32] Some subscribe to gossip and music industry folklore that Prince rejected the release of *The Black Album* after having a "bad trip" from ingesting ecstasy and seeing signs of its inherent evil properties.[33] For the record, ecstasy, an illegal recreational drug used to heighten feelings of pleasure, can trigger extreme paranoia.[34] But characterizing *The Black Album* as evil and its shelving as a form of preemptive protection for a vulnerable listening audience is too flimsy an explanation to account for the near total destruction of an album. To wholeheartedly accept such an argument feeds into the most strident characterizations of music, in general, and black music, in particular, as a source of moral and cultural decay. If so, then perhaps Tipper Gore and Susan Baker were spot on for founding the Parents Music Resource Center, an advocacy group that compelled the music industry to place Parental Advisory stickers on music judged too menacing for children to hear.

Indeed, modern examples abound of a variety of established musical acts openly flirting with and appearing to promote Satanism, like the Rolling Stones, Alice Cooper, Bones, Thugs and Harmony, and the rap group Three 6 Mafia. But casting music as "bad" and the principal source of social delinquency has a long history of unsubstantiated claims.[35] For example, evil intentions were ascribed to the blues as the "devil's music," and there is also the arcane superstition surrounding the dissonant tri-tone, deemed the devil's interval. If such superstitions are correct then Prince was right to protect the public from such negative music and have *The Black Album* destroyed.

In reality, *The Black Album* is not anymore "negative" than much of the material Prince had already released, along with subsequent music to come. In fact, Prince promoted a range of material a few years later that invited a variety of sided-eyed assessments concerning the "positive" value of his music. Case in point, Prince's dance track single, "Gett Off," from the *Diamonds and Pearls* (1991) studio album, promoted stranger sex, and at the 1991 MTV Video Music Awards show Prince performed the song in see-through pants that exposed his buttocks against the backdrop of a Caligula-like Roman orgy. Lastly, *The Black Album* was officially released in 1994, proving Prince relented on the strident conclusion that the music was too negative or evil for human ears to ever hear. In my mind, the misfire is not the music but the aesthetic choices. Besides the fact that, on an LP entitled *The Black Album*, Prince pines for Cindy Crawford, a white supermodel, and confesses he will pay money to have intercourse with her, a blatant affirmation of white beauty and black desire, there were more egregious aesthetic choices concerning race rooted in emerging notions of urban black racial authenticity.

Before *The Black Album* Prince had spent almost ten years as a quasi-black artist trying to outmaneuver the draconian racial politics of the music industry and the Jim Crow programming politics of early-1980s MTV. Admittedly, the racial ambiguities Prince invoked early in his career allowed him to successfully traverse a racially divided entertainment landscape, but after the apex of his career with *Purple Rain* Prince began to privilege, in earnest, a black music aesthetic following the *ATWD* release. *The Black Album* was a result of Prince privileging a black music aesthetic and with entirely black packaging; the literal look and name of the release signified a rebuke of Prince's former crossover image. In no uncertain terms, one listen to the album puts to rest any speculation about what the packaging or title suggested. Yet Prince's declaration of blackness on *The Black Album* included several sour notes toward hip-hop as an emergent music genre and budding black cultural movement.

At the time, 1987, the music industry and American pop culture were on the cusp of a radical transformation. Artists such as LL Cool J with *Bigger and Deffer*, Public Enemy with *Yo! Bum Rush the Show* (1987), Eric B. and Rakim with *Paid in Full* (1987), and KRS-One and DJ Scott La Rock's *Criminal Minded* (1987) led the charge of an emergent form of music that was unapologetically black and laden with urban street vernacular. The following year a music video program titled *Yo! MTV Raps* (1988–1995) provided an assortment of rap videos, in-studio performances, and interviews with rappers. The Golden Era of Hip-Hop was beginning, and blackness, vis-à-vis hip-hop, was now a significant component of programming on MTV now that black artists were no longer banned from prominent MTV video rotation. On *The Black Album* Prince appeared ambivalent, at best, concerning hip-hop.

Instead of embracing this insurgent sound on the verge of blazing, like a wild prairie fire, across the American pop culture landscape, *The Black Album* was hostile toward hip-hop.[36] For example, the third track of *The Black Album* is a tune titled "Dead on It." Even though Prince playfully delivers his lyrics the track is an angry diatribe against hip-hop: "I turned on my radio to hear some music play / I got a silly rapper talking silly shit instead / And the only good rapper is one that's dead . . . on it. See the rapper's problem usually stem from being tone deaf / Pack the house then try to sing / There won't be no one left." Prince clearly communicates his disdain for hip-hop and the talent quotient of any hip-hop MC. But like nearly everything with Prince, his relationship with hip-hop was complicated. On one track he disparages the genre, on another he tries to incorporate it. The song "Cindy C" showcases a female vocalist providing a mediocre example of rapping, while the track "Bob George" displays a glimmer of artistic originality for what the emergent genre could sound like when Prince was "dead on it." On "Bob George," Prince distorts his vocal pitch into a low menacing drawl and delivers a deluge of vulgarities to berate a woman he's holding hostage with a firearm. Later he declares his dislike for Prince as a "skinny motherfucker with the high voice." The basic, but catchy, hip-hop beat complements Prince's deep baritone voice perfectly and makes "Bob George," Prince's most aurally "authentic" hip-hop track he ever released.

At its best, "Bob George" demonstrated that Prince could take a genre that appeared the most incongruent with his sonic style, and make it his own, a feat similar to "Sister," with punk-rock, on the *Dirty Mind* album. At its worst, "Bob George" was a sonic caricature of hip-hop in which Prince presented a hip-hop persona that comported with retrograde notions of black men as criminals, misogynistic, and prone to violence. In this sense, even when Prince was bad he was good. Similar to the punk movement of the past, that Prince pulled from early in his career, with "Bob George" Prince evoked the insurgent style hip-hop offered along with the genre's artistic leeway for nihilistic sentiments. Prince tapped into and expressed these transgressive impulses in "Bob George" before misogynistic objectification and senseless violence became mainstreamed and a dominant trend throughout the 1990s with gangster rap, a mode of misogynistic representation epitomized several years later on the successful rap record release *Doggystyle* (1993).

Ultimately, even without the hip-hop miscues, *The Black Album* was underdone. Too often the lyrics were insipid and uninspired. Nonetheless, as a bootleg, *The Black Album* grew in lore over the years. When *The Black Album* was finally and officially released, seven years later, it was more musty than funky. The tracks sounded like stale outtakes from a Time album that never got made after their break-up. Arguably, one can engage in endless speculation over what facilitated the shelving of *The Black Album*. Nonetheless, one fact stands out, *The Black Album* marks the onset of Prince's struggle to situate hip-hop alongside his "Minneapolis sound."

With *Sign o' the Times* Prince had firmly established himself as a musical innovator and proven he possessed an uncanny ability to assimilate sonic genres and make them his own. Prince first demonstrated how he was a sonic innovator when he embraced the synthesizer-laden elements of new wave to create his own genre-defying fusion of new wave, rock, and soul during the early 1980s. Even Prince's derivative and cloying *Around the World in a Day*, with its Beatles-like psychedelic trappings, deserves an "A" for effort for showing how Prince was relentless in refashioning his signature sound and style. Only Prince would deliver an experimental art-rock release at the height of mainstream popular success.

Given how hip-hop articulated an almost fetishistic attachment to black urban racial authenticity it made for an ill-fitting genre for Prince to match. Recall that, for over a decade Prince's "Minneapolis sound" represented a racially integrated look and sound. Not surprisingly, hip-hop proved more difficult for Prince to successfully absorb. Much of the 1990s saw Prince chasing hip-hop trends and reacting to them, a mode that marked the beginning of a chaotic period of fluctuating achievements for Prince as a popular musician and forecast a series of missteps, trails, tribulations, and the release of another terrible film.

5

Chaos and Crossroads

> Everybody can't be on top / But life it
> ain't real funky, unless it's got that pop
> —Prince, *Pop Life*

> Rap is not pop / If you call it that then
> stop
> —Q-Tip, *Check the Rhyme*

Lovesexy (1988) was Prince's eleventh studio album (counting *The Black Album*). Most notably, *Lovesexy* replaced the shelved *The Black Album*. The latter was in homage to James Brown's funk soul brother style of music. The former launched into uncharted sonic territory as a new age gospel funk LP, where Prince proselytized about love and provided feeble sermons warning listeners about the "spooky electric." On this release the topic of sex took a backseat to spiritual awareness. Perhaps Prince was totally spent after having/giving so many simulated orgasms on his previous LPs. Accordingly, there was a listless undercurrent to the album even though *Lovesexy* sounded like a slicker (possibly overproduced) version of the sonic chaos perfected on the *Parade* release. The *Lovesexy* album cover also hinted at creative fatigue even though it attracted the type of controversy befitting a more original depiction. The outside cover displayed a nude Prince sitting inside a giant orchid with his legs strategically crossed to cover his genital region, an image that prompted some retailers not to stock the album.[1] In reality, the cover was rather mundane and definitively repetitive.

Prince had done the nude photograph with his penis strategically hidden twice already. The first time was on the inside jacket sleeve of the *For You* LP, where a nude Prince is sitting on a bed holding a guitar strategically placed to block his genitals from view. The second time was on the back cover of the *Prince* release where Prince is naked while straddling a white horse with wings. For those in the know, the *Lovesexy* cover was Prince repeating himself, a sure sign of creative exhaustion. In addition, he included a track originally found on *The Black Album*, the saccharin slow jam "When 2 R in Love." As the 1990s fast approached, not only was Prince cannibalizing his own work, a harbinger that Prince had run out of new ideas, he was also relinquishing his role as a sonic gadfly, and his worst creative inclination toward hip-hop cropped up on *Lovesexy*—bad rapping.

On "Alphabet St.," the hottest single of the entire nine-track *Lovesexy* release, Prince started to rap. "Alphabet St." was a catchy, hook-driven track that reached #3 on the R&B Top Ten Singles chart and showcased Prince performing an abbreviated rap that concludes with Prince shrieking, "Cat, I need you to rap." Cat completes her odd succession of rhymed verses by imploring listeners to, "jerk your body like a horny pony would." For any hip-hop aficionados that heard Cat's admonishment, their most likely body movement might have been shaking their head from side-to-side signaling no, not only to the request but also to hearing any more attempts by Prince or Cat to rap. Without a doubt, "Alphabet St." was an earnest effort to incorporate hip-hop into Prince's sonic repertoire. Most likely, the performance was hamstrung by the fact that Cat Glover was a talented dancer and choreographer and not an MC. As a consequence, quickly passing the mic to her to "spit bars," in the parlance of hip-hop, was a task tailor made for failure.

Of course, having a "true MC" as a guest rapper was not mandatory for a track to have musical merit as an authentic expression of hip-hop.[2] Deborah Harry, the female lead singer of the all-white new wave band Blondie, "rapped" on "Rapture," a song off the group's *Autoamerican* (1980) LP. Harry rapped about a man from Mars that eats cars, bars, and people. The rap passage was just as zany as the one offered on "Alphabet St." Nevertheless, by Harry using hip-hop catchphrases like "sure-shot," "hip-hop," and "fly," her

Dadaist ramblings were grounded in an authentic hip-hop sensibility. Harry also slyly name-checked Grandmaster Flash and Fab 5 Freddy, two pioneering figures in the emergent genre. As a result, "Rapture" solidified Harry's position as a progressive and insurgent presence in hip-hop lore.[3] Blondie's song shot up the charts to become a number 1 hit. When Prince incorporated rap on his *Lovesexy* release, he was unable to tap into the art of rapping just the mechanical form. Nevertheless, "Alphabet St." demonstrated how Prince wanted to expand his musical vocabulary to include hip-hop, and the song marks Prince publicly conceding to the power and popularity of the genre.

Unfortunately, Prince seemed committed to augmenting his music with only substandard rappers. Perhaps having Morris Day and The Time upstage him in the past made Prince leery of working with a rapper that could move the crowd in a manner he could not. The lack of quality control hampered Prince's ability to establish bona fide hip-hop credentials and contributed to a perception that hip-hop was more of a gimmick to gain contemporary relevancy and a means to boost his slumping record sells in order to reestablish his pop music dominance.[4] Prince's next music project proved fortuitous in this regard. He provided the soundtrack for Tim Burton's neo-camp film version of the Dark Knight entitled *Batman* (1989).

The Prince soundtrack for the superhero film was named the same as the film and placed Prince in the middle of a marketing dynamo that reinvigorated his dithering record sells. The commercial thrust, gross commodification, and overarching promotion strategy associated with *Batman* made it less a film and more of a commercial to penetrate various consumer markets that ranged from toys to everyday household items, such as bedding.[5] Accordingly, Prince's *Batman* album appeared more as a tie-in for Tim Burton's film than a self-generated studio album meant to satiate public demand. In this sense, Prince's *Batman* album was a blatant promotional project and proved another example of Prince at his crossover best. The breakout single from the nine-track release was "Batdance," a #1 hit single.[6]

On "Batdance" Prince employed his own take on hip-hop break-beat turntablism, a particular style of hip-hop DJing whereby a DJ mixes creative sound effects from two or more different albums. Grandmaster Flash first pioneered this style on a track entitled "The Adventures of Grandmaster Flash on the Wheels of Steel." For "Batdance" Prince used snippets of dialogue from Burton's *Batman* film, remixed the popular refrain from the *Batman* (1966–1968) television theme song, and dropped a wicked breakbeat halfway through the track. The patchwork of voices and snippets from other hit songs woven into "Batdance" epitomized Prince, at his best, absorbing another genre's sonic calling card and making it his own. The video for the single "Batdance" played in heavy rotation on MTV and "over the radio, 'Batdance' and other cuts from Prince's *Batman* album got strong play on rock stations and 'crossed over' for similarly strong play on black radio stations."[7]

"Batdance" the song was serious. "Batdance" the music video was silly. At one point in the music video, Prince crawls on his knees between the legs of five blonde white women proclaiming, "I wanna bust that body." All the same and in retrospect, the pop (read white music audience) success of *Batdance*, proved Prince could meet the white pop-rock crowd and still reach the black music market with a catchy groove. Most interestingly, "Batdance" demonstrated Prince's successful deployment of a hip-hop music aesthetic and proved Prince could embrace hip-hop and make hit songs, an embrace that had major ramifications for Prince's career and black music. For a moment, Prince was a black artist whose body of work provided a bulwark against the hip-hop tidal wave gathering momentum in the distance. To this point, music critic Michaelangelo Matos went so far as to write that *Sign o' the Times* was "the last classic R&B album prior to hip-hop's takeover of black music and the final four-sided blockbuster of the vinyl era."[8] Eventually, even Prince conceded to the power of hip-hop.

In the wake of the success of *Batman* Prince faced a fork in the road. Prince could continue pushing the envelope with idiosyncratic forward-looking material or move to make more pop-oriented songs informed by hip-hop, an increasingly dominant music form at the time. Prince chose the latter. Unfortunately, for every successful step Prince took forward that captured the feel and sound of hip-hop, like with "Batdance," he took two steps backward. Case in point, *Graffiti Bridge* (1990), a crummy little film peddled as the sequel to *Purple Rain*, is a prime example of how Prince could be completely tone-deaf when it came to hip-hop. Sure, *Graffiti Bridge* brought back all the players from *Purple Rain*, and continued the battle of the bands theme from the original movie. Yet *Graffiti Bridge* had very little in common with *Purple Rain*. As a film, *Graffiti Bridge* is unwatchable. As a train wreck, it has its moments.

Prince and his New Power Generation band battle Morris and his band, The Time, for full ownership of the club. For some reason, the previous owner of the business gave each musician half ownership of the venue. The film presents a variety of lame musical face-offs between the two bands to decide the winner of the club. Interestingly, a rapper named T.C. (T.C. Ellis), is repeatedly shown lingering off stage for his chance to rap alongside The Kid (Prince). By the end of the film, as the credits roll, T.C. performs his rap, an odd bookend when compared to *Purple Rain* and *Under the Cherry Moon*. *Purple Rain* closed out the film with two encore Prince performances. *Under the Cherry Moon* ended with a music video of Prince and his band performing the song "Mountains," as the credit rolls. With *Graffiti Bridge* Prince is only shown sitting at a keyboard terminal with his back to the audience. Prince literally ends the film by turning his back to the audience while a rapper holds center stage, a conclusion in stark contrast to all of Prince's previous films. Ostensibly, once you get past the bad poetry, cheap sets, and dreadful acting, *Graffiti Bridge* telegraphed that hip-hop was the cornerstone of Prince's new sound moving forward.

The first wave of Prince's rap onslaught started with the release of *Diamonds and Pearls* (1991), his fourteenth studio album. The album showcased Prince aping the new jack swing of Teddy Riley and playing his strongest hip-hop hand with the lead single "Gett Off," a track that included sampling, rapping, and a bass-heavy beat. On the one hand, "Gett Off" was such a standout dance track that Prince's rapping was like a background effect in comparison to the song's driving beat. On the other hand, the rapping on songs such as "Jughead" and "Push" was so amateurish and shrill it made Shawn Brown's "Rapping Duke" (1984, a rap song based on Brown impersonating the voice of a deceased John Wayne) sound like a masterpiece.

Prince's rapping skills showed few signs of improvement since "Alphabet St.," and, worst of all, his grasp of the genre grew increasingly derivative. Take, for example, the music video for the single "Sexy M.F." The video showed Prince rapping into a gold-plated microphone shaped like a gun, while three black men flanked Prince, standing around high-end exotic sports cars, and a black woman (Troy Beyer) paraded around them in a bikini wearing a see thru blouse. The video had all the tropes of a hip-hop video; expensive cars, black men posturing, the objectification of "light skinned" women, and various camera shots of buttocks dancing into the camera. Interestingly, in the "Sexy M.F." music video the camera spends as much time recording men shaking their behind as the women, an amusing point of departure from conventional hip-hop videos.

The image of Prince in the extended music video for "Gangster Glam (1991)" was less derivative but even more dissonant. One viewing of Prince in the "Gangster Glam" music video clearly demonstrates that Prince is no gangster. First of all, the music video shows Prince doing pushups by his pool in ill-fitting swim attire, and roller-skating. Who knew Prince could skate? Ultimately, the behind-the-scenes images in "Gangster Glam" made the music video look more like a cheerful home movie than a hardcore exposé on inner-city street life. As a consequence, Prince's appropriation of gangster rap was stymied on two fronts. First, the aesthetic bread and butter of hip-hop is street authenticity, and, even though Prince had plenty of swagger, his street credibility was sorely lacking.

"Gangster rap," was predicated on a powerful conceit; the gangster rapper was describing, if not endorsing, a hyperbolic world of urban violence, pathological behavior, hypermaterialism, and a nihilistic outlook. Although the language and imagery were fraught with hyperbole they were considered real. Against the strident cultural politics of racial authenticity found in "gangsta rap" the transformation of Prince from a crossover pop star into a gangster-pimp-daddy reeked of manufactured artificiality. Prince did not offer a convincing and authentic rendering of any inner-city tough guy. While promoting "Gett Off" Prince had worn pants on MTV with the backside cut out showing his ass. This was not gangster. Never was, never will be, a conclusion that leads directly to the second point. Hip-hop was an incongruent fit with the gender-fluid style Prince had established for decades.

Prince's strongest role was playing the part of a lithe androgynous doe-eyed pixie that fused all types of music genres with sexual fantasy. Prince was too unique to let his image be dictated and defined by a gold-plated gun-microphone. Early in his career Prince often signified his potential queerness via affected mannerisms and coded performances. For just over a decade, Prince had established himself as a sexual outlaw whose bad boy aura was enhanced by a willingness to demonstrate and feel comfortable expressing his feminine qualities. In the early 1990s hip-hop had little to no room for a gender-fluid performer like Prince.

Like the rap group P.M. Dawn, rappers closer to Prince in style and sound faced extreme prejudice and marginalization. P.M. Dawn released several hit singles on their two consecutive albums *Of the Heart, of the Soul and of the Cross: The Utopian Experience* (1991) and *The Bliss Album . . . ?* (1993). Coincidently, the lead rapper of P.M. Dawn went by the moniker Prince Be and was seen as such a disgrace to "true" hip-hop by the rapper KRS-One that he chased Prince Be off the stage of his own show. Then, to add further insult, he replaced the P.M. Dawn set list with his hit songs. Such draconian reactions to alternative articulations of hip-hop affirmed stereo-typical notions of hip-hop masculinity as aggressive posturing prone to vio-lent confrontation. Rap music and its adherents too often conflated black hypermasculinity and black female objectification (along with misogynis-tic impulses) as a cornerstone of authentic "blackness," a sensibility on full display with groups like 2 Live Crew and Sir Mix-a-Lot's double platinum ode to women with big behinds, "Baby Got Back" (1992).

Admittedly, in the not so distant past, the free and full expression of black masculinity in America had an abhorrent history, particularly when white women were the subjects of real or imagined attention.[9] Accordingly, it is not surprising that a black male crossover artist like Little Richard, singing to white crowds filled with screaming adolescent white women, emoted a queer persona to dampen the full sexual current generated by his music in 1950s America. Even several decades later, when Marvin Gaye had the cross-over hit song "Sexual Healing (1982)," wherein he proclaimed he was "hot just like an oven . . . you're my medicine / open up and let me in," Gaye dressed up black desire in tuxedoed elegance for the music video of the hit song. How a black artist looked could calm or agitate white America's appre-hensions concerning black male sexuality. Without a doubt, compared to the past and in the field of mainstream access, Prince was able to make amaz-ing incursions into American popular culture, considering his in your face sex junkie act. Nonetheless, the coded queerness Prince exuded also worked to subvert the very racial anxieties it aroused. I wonder, for an artist overly preoccupied with outmaneuvering the racial restrictions at work in the late 1970s and throughout the 1980s, if hip-hop seduced Prince to overvalue the genre as a source of self-expression and a conduit of unabridged cultural blackness?

Without question, in the early 1990s, there was something different about Prince and his relationship with hip-hop than with other music genres he was able to incorporate on previous albums. An assortment of Prince's for-mer studio engineers and his legendary tour manager, Alan Leeds, attest to the seemingly existential crisis hip-hop generated for Prince as he struggled to come to terms with the popularity of the genre by trying to rap.[10] Regard-less of the existential quandary, commercial motivation, or racial leeway hip-hop presented to Prince the genre was an incongruent fit with the gender-fluid style and representational politics Prince signified.

Eventually, the draconian notion of "real" hip-hop subsided, and it did not matter if "gangsta rap" was real or imaginary because it was profitable.

It was disco all over again, whereby a slew of dissimilar artists tried to cash in on a profitable music craze, a formula that reached its farcical limits when Broadway singer Ethel Merman began belching out disco versions of old show tunes she had made famous in the 1930s. Merman was a Broadway legend, but her "disco" songs sounded contrived, and they underscored commercial pandering at its worst. Similarly, MC Hammer, the sensational dancing rapper known for wearing "genie pants," gave "gangsta" rap a shot. MC Hammer's *Funky Headhunter* (1994) release demonstrated how quickly gangster rap became a gimmick to cash in on. Prince seemed similarly situated with his gangster glam interpretation of gangster rap.

Despite the dissimilar polarities between Prince and hip-hop, the Prince "rap" offensive continued. The *Love Symbol* (1992) release had Prince, Tony M., or both men "rapping" on nine of the sixteen songs—rough. On *Symbol* Prince also sampled from other songs. Think about that for a minute. Prince, one of the most original musicians of the modern era, a multi-instrumentalist, an artist that made music for a variety of other artists, and a composer of so much music that he kept hundreds, possibly more than a thousand, compositions locked away in a "vault," was sampling someone else's music trying to make a hit record. For the moment, it seemed like Prince had forgotten he was too unique to let his image be dictated and defined by a gold-plated gun-microphone and "hard" beats. Prince, at his best, symbolized a more multidimensional expression of black racial and sexual identity, a black weirdo music nerd that was cool. Most importantly, black folk that declared themselves Prince fans were making a tacit affirmation that they themselves were different too.

Eventually, hip-hop broadened beyond urban exploits and sexual candor. Groups such as *Arrested Development*, on their debut release *3 Years, 5 Months and 2 Days in the Life Of...* (1992), garnered widespread critical acclaim with their Afrocentric image and socially conscious lyrical content, the antithesis of gangster rap. All the same, Prince did not drape himself with overt cultural cues of renewed Afrocentric pride or articulate brash racial critiques. Socially conscious relevant rap was also an ill fit for Prince, even though some of his more didactic material like *Goldnigga* (1993), a Prince-produced LP of music by his New Power Generation touring band. tried to fill the bill. This is not to say, in the wake of the Rodney King beating, that Prince remained neutral to the cresting racial awareness of the early 1990s.

The *Diamonds and Pearls* (1991) release contained "Money Don't Matter 2 Night," a poignant song and source for a gem of a music video directed by Spike Lee. Prince asked Spike Lee, a prolific black filmmaker and one of America's most prominent racial provocateurs, to create the video for "Money Don't Matter 2 Night." The only catch was that Prince would not be in the video. In Prince's place Lee depicted a poor African American household struggling to stay optimistic during dire economic times. The video begins with the father, breaking the fourth wall, questioning the president of the United States about the lack of employment opportunities he faces and, by extension, black men in general. Next, a montage of stock footage clips of American wealth and poverty are paired with Prince's song. There is a sensitive and introspective quality to the scenes depicting the parents and children gathering around the dinner table, a black family striving to preserve their humanity in the face of economic strife.

The second version of the "Money Don't Matter 2 Night" video intercut footage of Prince and his NPG band members performing the song with images from the first version of Lee's video. Both videos were powerful, but the latter made an explicit connection between Prince, poverty, blackness, and the politics of racial inequality in America. The optics of the video were undeniable. Prince rested in the center of a music video that openly criticized the American racial and economic order of the day. "Money Don't Matter 2 Night" was one of Prince's most socially conscious expression of black racial awareness in front of and behind the camera. Prince pledged the proceeds from the single to the United Negro College Fund to enhance educational opportunities at private historically black colleges and universities.[11] All of that said, Prince's next racial statement was, arguably, his most severe misstep.

In 1993, Prince penciled "Slave" across his cheek to protest his music contract with Warner Bros. Records and turned a private feud with his record label into a public controversy that brought attention to Prince's racial politics and his own degree of racial consciousness. By penciling "Slave" across his cheek, to denote his status with the record label, Prince appeared to promote an awkward racial equivalency whereby his protracted contractual standoff with a corporate employer, as a black multimillionaire, was similar to racial oppression in America under a system of enslavement. Simply stated, once upon a time in America, black folk were enslaved and systematically exploited as commodities divested of their humanity, hopes, dreams, and labor. Certainly, exploitation of recording artists by their corporate

masters is not a novelty in the recording industry. Moreover, black recording artists are not strangers to contractual shenanigans.[12] But by Prince
appearing in public with the word "Slave" written on the side of his face he
was culturally and politically tone deaf. Rick James, years prior to Prince's
outrage, provided a better model of corporate resistance when James took
his personal dilemma with MTV rejecting his videos and broadened its
application to address why MTV discriminated against an entire genre of
black music.

When Prince penciled "Slave" across his cheek it was meant to bring public shame to Warner Bros. Records, but it made Prince look selfish, out of
touch, and willing to use a horrible historical period for African Americans
as a publicity stunt intended solely to benefit his career. In fact, Prince's issue
with Warner Bros. Records had less to do with race and more to do with
profit. Basically, Prince was too prolific. Prince had released fourteen studio albums in the twelve years since the debut of *For You* (1978). From the
record label's perspective, Prince was saturating the market with music, and
it diminished the value of his material. Moreover, each Prince release
required the record label to commit a sizable outlay of expenditures on production, manufacturing, and promotional marketing. Accordingly, the
Warner record label eventually adopted a more strident position with Prince
and halted the release of Prince's new material at such a fast clip. As a consequence, a relationship that began as beneficial and mutually respectful
changed to one filled with contentiousness and recrimination.

Without a doubt, Prince's symbolic ploy was an overreach, but he was
not entirely unfounded for trying to, literally, draw attention to the racial
politics of the music industry. Prince's sense of economic exploitation by the
recording industry was not without merit. The record company Prince
signed with owned his original music recordings (in recording industry
nomenclature they are called masters), a situation shared by a multitude of
other music artists. By scrawling "Slave" across his face he was trying to high-
light the unfair nature of the relationship in which, to quote Prince, "If
you don't own your masters, then your masters own you." What Prince's
wordplay alluded to was a lack of proprietorship, a point of reflection that
tapped into a deep and lingering tension in the African American experience and the black popular imagination.

During American enslavement African Americans lacked ownership of
their own bodies and the products of their labor. In this sense, proprietorship is part and parcel of the African American struggle for full citizenship

in American society, a point given critical expression in works like Lorraine Hansberry's acclaimed play *A Raisin in the Sun* (1959) and the entirety of works by Pulitzer Prize–winning playwright August Wilson. But Prince was not a slave, and a lopsided economic relationship with a mainstream record label is not even close to anything associated with slavery. Prince was a multimillion-dollar musician. Perhaps a better racial metaphor to explain his (and by implication) other musicians' predicament in the American music industry is sharecropping.

On the heels of African American emancipation, southern planters devised a system called sharecropping whereby recently freed blacks were granted credit so they could purchase materials to farm a plot of land on the plantation they had formerly been enslaved on. Former slaves split the profits from their seasonal crops with their former owners, along with paying for the cost of using farm materials and provisions, a formula that resulted in black folk mired in debt and unable to buy the land they tilled.[13] Similarly, new recording artists are often offered a large amount of money, projected against future royalties, to sign with a major record label. In turn, the artists are billed for recording costs and various services fees for completing a predetermined number of releases, but they never own their recorded material. In this sense, Prince was trying to make a valid point about the exploitative nature of the relationship between artists and major record labels. Nonetheless, appearing in public and performing on stage with "Slave" scrawled across his cheek was a failure of execution. Despite this obvious misfire and example of a reckless spectacle Prince engaged in more symbolic shenanigans. Prince changed his name to an unpronounceable glyph. So much for the angry declarative song entitled "My Name is Prince (1992)." He was now known as, "The artist formerly known as Prince."

The use of a glyph to replace Prince's name was just another stunt to chide his record label. The rationale was that if Prince was a slave to contractual obligations, then "symbol man" had no agreements to honor and could do whatever he wanted. If not that, at least Prince could generate less than glowing press about Warner Bros. Records. What did occur was Prince chose to release a series of perfunctory albums just to satisfy his contractual obligations. The Prince "quickie" LP releases were the lackluster *Come* (1994), a re-released *The Black Album* (1994), the choleric *The Gold Experience* (1995), and the disjointed *Chaos and Disorder* (1996), a junk album.[14] These albums only fulfilled contractual obligations. As meaningful music they were underwhelming and marked a cold streak of hit-and-miss music. Sure, Prince churned out periodic singles that charted, but his overall material during this spate of required releases was inconsistent and second-rate by almost any standard. Ultimately, by releasing mediocre material Prince did not damage the record company; rather he alienated his audience and distanced himself from his fans.[15] In short, Prince cut off his nose to spite his face.

Prince's battle with his record label consumed him and served as a catalyst for making mediocre music, a surefire way to court claims of his being a has-been. Admittedly, Prince's choices were limited, and his decision to churn out a series of "quickie" albums contained a degree of rational pragmatism. Prince would have done himself a favor to revisit the career of the legendary soul singer Marvin Gaye who, in the late 1970s, faced a similar contractual predicament as Prince. Gaye agreed to have the royalties of his next album given directly to his former wife as part of their divorce settlement. The stage was set for Marvin to take a pragmatic posture for how much creative energy and investment he was willing to dedicate to an album meant only to fulfill a contractual obligation. Gaye states, "I figured I'd just do a 'quickie' record—nothing heavy, nothing even good. Why should I break my neck when Anna was going to wind up with the money anyway? But the more I lived with the notion, the more it fascinated. Besides, I owed the public my best effort. Finally, I did the record [*Hear, My Dear* (1978)] out of deep passion."[16] In 1978 *Hear, My Dear* was released and initially received lukewarm reviews with only a handful willing to declare it was good given that it sounded nothing like previous Gaye albums.[17] In subsequent decades, however, the achingly honest double album was affirmed as possibly his best work.[18] *Hear, My Dear* illustrates Gaye's commitment to art over commerce.

In contrast to Gaye, Prince was unable to successfully address the commerce versus art dilemma with Gaye's level of artistic grace. The spate of mediocre contractually conceded releases chipped away at Prince's standing as a relevant force in the music industry during the late 1990s. The only positive takeaway from Prince's symbolic gambit and creative misstep is it provided the onus for Prince to establish his own record label. But the damage was done. With the name change, Prince literally disappeared, and in his absence emerged a deep yearning for the Prince of the past, before he became "The Artist." This nostalgic impulse concerning Prince crops up in Spike Lee's *Girl 6* (1996), a film ostensibly about an aspiring African American actress that decides to address her money needs by becoming a phone sex worker and gradually loses her grip on reality. Thematically speaking, the focus on the interplay between female sexuality and mental fitness invokes Roman Polanski's disturbingly brilliant film *Repulsion* (1965). But in an unexpected way *Girl 6* is most concerned with black nostalgia, and Prince rests at the aesthetic center of the film's turn toward the past.

The opening of *Girl 6* signals that it is a backward-looking film by duplicating a scene from *Fame* (1980), a film about several freshman students at a prestigious performing arts high school in New York City. One of the most disconcerting scenes from *Fame* occurs toward the conclusion of the film and involves a young female student who is duped into doing a screen test for an amateur pornographer claiming to be a legitimate film director. The scene unfolds from the perspective of the pornographer as he bullies Coco (Irene Cara) to remove her top. He records her as she exposes her breast, all the while sobbing her way through the porn dialogue. *Girl 6* repeats the scene by depicting Judy (Theresa Randall), a young African American actress, in a videotaped audition, where she is pressured to remove her blouse. Judy reluctantly exposes her breast then abruptly walks out of the audition.

Both depictions are sober representations of the exploitative objectification of women in the entertainment industry. Yet Lee's lifting of the scene portends a fetish for the black pop culture of the past and is clearly articulated through a variety of bygone films and TV shows shoehorned into *Girl 6* as imaginary skits. Judy makes appearances as Dorothy Dandridge in *Carmen Jones* (1954), as Pam Grier in a generic blaxploitation film, and as a female guest on the black television sitcom *The Jeffersons* (1975–1985), and, toward the film's finale, Judy is depicted as a 1940s Hollywood glamor queen. Nonetheless, the real lost object of Lee's nostalgic affection is not these foregrounded examples of black popular culture from the past but the idealized object playing in the background throughout the film—Prince.

The soundtrack for *Girl 6* contained only songs by Prince, and most of it material from his musical heyday. Out of the thirteen tracks only five songs were from 1992 or later. Conceptually, no matter what decade the songs originated from, having a Prince soundtrack for a film examining the erotic realms of sex-talk and kink makes perfect sense given that Prince created and cornered the market on graphic sex-talk and music. But in reality, most of Prince's 1980s material was an awkward counterpoint, in general, to the style of the late 1990s and, in particular, the actions depicted in the film. As a result, Lee's choice to have only Prince songs playing in the background proved more anachronistic than innovative. The nostalgic impulse telegraphed in *Girl 6* fell flat, and the soundtrack for the film promoted the idea that Prince's best material was behind him. But the nostalgic impulse and recycled music used for *Girl 6* were part and parcel of a broader aesthetic crisis facing black music during the mid-1990s.

Nelson George, in *The Death of Rhythm and Blues* (1988), proclaimed that R&B was creatively bankrupt in the late 1980s. By the 1990s George's post-mortem prediction appeared quite prescient given how new chart-topping hip-hop artists of the 1990s recycled old R&B-sampled loops to fuel the popularity of various hit songs. For example, MC Hammer's "U Can't Touch This" (1990), Biggie Smalls's "Juicy" (1994), Coolio's "Gangsta's Paradise" (1995), and Method Man's "I'll Be There For You/You're All I Need To Get By" (1995) suffered from sonic cannibalism of old hit songs. This trend affirmed George's prognosis that the best of black music had already been made. In addition, many of the new successful R&B artists of the 1990s did not even play instruments. Chart-topping acts like Boys II Men, Mary J. Blige, Usher, Mariah Carey, TLC, Dru Hill, and Toni Braxton were perpetually tethered to studio producers and various songwriters for their success. But as the sermon admonishes, "beware of premature autopsies."[19] Contrary to George's proclamation R&B was not dead. Rather, an emergent black music genre, called neo-soul, helped to resuscitate R&B and introduce the world to Michael Eugene Archer (stage name D' Angelo).

Neo-soul was a repurposed form of R&B that combined hip-hop rhythms with accomplished instrumentation, and D'Angelo was the flagship artist of the emergent genre. In 1995, the twenty-one-year-old musical wunderkind quietly dropped *Brown Sugar*. There were no "old school" R&B-sampled grooves to lure music fans in to check out the new release. Just D'Angelo playing his keyboard with a bluesy jazz lilt and singing in a sweet falsetto, a style that was one part seduction and two parts sanctified preacher. Unlike Prince's debut release, *For You*, D'Angelo's introduction to the music industry achieved platinum-selling status and garnered acclaim from music critics and fans alike. Because D'Angelo, like Prince, wrote, produced, and performed on his debut release an LP filled with soulful instrumentality, Prince-like falsetto vocals, deep baselines, and a pair of intoxicating bedroom eyes, D'Angelo was judged as picking up where Prince had fallen off.

A few years earlier, Lenny Kravitz was positioned to be a Prince proxy given his musical chops as a writer, performer, and producer. Moreover, Kravitz's sophomore release, *Mama Said* (1991), had all the trappings of a Prince record and sensibility with its eclectic mixing of pop, soul, and psychedelic tones. Except Kravitz's fuzzy retro-rock-centric music reeked of derivative guitar riffs and arrangements that made him more of a watered-down Jimi Hendrix wannabe than a Prince acolyte. In the end, Prince was too much of an original for Kravitz, and Kravitz sounded and drew too much from prior popular soundscapes. D'Angelo, in contrast, successfully integrated the popular hip-hop sound of the moment, making him a fresh voice to hear.[20] D'Angelo smoothed over and polished the jagged edge of hip-hop beats, accented them with soulful keyboard inflections, and added rolling bass rhythms. The result was an album that was both indebted to Prince and setting the stage for claims that D'Angelo was not only taking the Prince sound to the next level but replacing him, a point brashly argued in the liner notes of D'Angelo's second studio release, *Voodoo* (2000).

For the liner notes on the *Voodoo* album, Saul Williams, an acclaimed slam-poet and performance artist in his own right, was the designated scribe for sanctioning the importance of *Voodoo*. Williams literally waxed poetic on the merits and mission of D'Angelo's artistry in relationship to Prince:

Nowadays, I find my peers more inspired by an artist's business tactics than their artistry. In fact, we do not seem to mind an artistry that suffers in the face of seemingly good business. More artists seem to yearn to own their own labels, etc., than they seem to yearn to master their crafts. No, we cannot allow any more Bessie Smiths to occur, but once an artist owns their own publishing the question then becomes, what are you going to publish?

You might respond, "Lyrics? Yo, I can't even understand half the shit that D'Angelo be saying. That nigga sounds like Bobby McFerrin on opium." And I'd say, "You're right. Neither can I. But I am drawn to figure out what it is that he's saying. His vocal collaging intrigues me." Or you might say, "But his shit don't sound all that original, he just sounds like he's trying to be Prince or some shit." And I'd say, maybe you're right. At times he does. We often study the breathing techniques of our inspirations (inspire means to breathe in or to make breath, inhale).

The difference is that D'Angelo has allowed influence to simply take its place among his own intuitive artistry. He works to find his own voice within his many influences. I'd pay to see Prince's face as he listens to this album (Ahmir, of The Roots, said that the Artist lets Black people call him Prince). Do you think he'd feel robbed or inspired? My opinion, over the years as I've sat in countless conversations about why it is that the Artist puts out half the shit he does (you know the half I'm talking about) is because he lacks any new inspiration.

With *Voodoo* any coincidental comparisons between Prince and D'Angelo ceased. Rather, outright claims of the upstart replacing the master musician began, a point Williams's diatribe makes clear.

In terms of imagery, D'Angelo also invited blatant comparisons to Prince. For example, the music video for D'Angelo's "Me and Those Dreamin' Eyes of Mine," showed him, through the power of special effects, simultaneously singing and playing multiple instruments; bass guitar, drums, keyboards, and lead guitar. This was similar to the special effects used on the video for Prince's first hit song "I Wanna Be Your Lover," that showed Prince simultaneously playing multiple instruments and singing. But at the most visceral level the music video for D'Angelo's "Untitled (How Does It Feel)," from the *Voodoo* release, stoked Prince comparisons by several fold. The video begins with D'Angelo crooning directly into the camera as the camera slowly pans across his face, gradually pulling out to reveal his naked torso; toned and tight. The camera stops a fraction of a millimeter above where his groin begins. The visual impression is that D'Angelo is singing the slow simmering ballad naked. As he sings he periodically glances down, further suggesting just out of camera shot, and right below his waistline, someone is performing fellatio on him. When D'Angelo hits the climatic high note of the song he apparently is made to orgasm.

The "Untitled (How Does It Feel)" music video was a voyeuristic spectacle of optic wanderlust with D'Angelo playing the part of a black Adonis, a part that propelled D'Angelo into the realm of sex symbol and, for many, solidified him as the musical and sexual heir to Prince.[21] Prince relied on bare-chested pictures on his albums and posing nude with various objects shielding his genitals to signal how sex and the erotic were fused with his persona. But compared to D'Angelo these Prince depictions were static softcore promotional pinup images, representations that could never reach the fever-pitched climax the "Untitled (How Does It Feel)" music video literally achieved with D'Angelo. In short order, however, D'Angelo demonstrated he was not Prince and could not sustain, or did not want to continue stoking, the public's libido with more sexual antics. After *Voodoo* D'Angelo promptly disappeared and entered into a career-induced fog of depression, drug abuse, and sloth. When he returned to the public stage, after a nearly fifteen-year hiatus, his physique was no longer ripped and ready. Nonetheless, his music chops remained tight and on point. His long-awaited follow-up studio album to *Voodoo* was *Black Messiah* (2014), a soulful and brilliant work that unambiguously made clear that D'Angelo is an artist's artist.

In the end, D'Angelo was less an heir or replacement for Prince and more a benefactor of Prince's sexual showmanship and superb musicianship. Of course hindsight is twenty-twenty, and, even though imitation is the sincerest form of flattery, it is quite clear that D'Angelo was no Prince. Just by comparing their respective output alone, there is no contest. D'Angelo's creative productivity would stall for sixteen years after *Voodoo* and, as of this writing, D'Angelo has released only three studio albums over two decades. Prince released thirty-nine studio albums over thirty-seven years. Moreover, if not for Prince, the type of sexual excess suggested in D'Angelo's albatross of a video, "Untitled (How Does It Feel)" would have been unthinkable as mainstream entertainment. But it was also unfair to compare D'Angelo to Prince in the same way that it is unfair to compare apples to oranges.

Even though each man could deliver the sexual sizzle, sing in falsetto, and render himself emotionally vulnerable, D'Angelo, unlike Prince, was able to augment his erotically constructed aura with traditional tropes of hip-hop masculinity, a cornrow hairstyle, requisite baggy denim pants, and Timberland boots. For Prince, androgynous costuming, use of makeup, and a hairstyle that accentuated Prince's effeminate sexual pose dampened Prince's masculinity quotient. Prince's bad boy sexual aura was infused by cross-dressing performativity, a quality that made him an exotic novelty and hinted at erotic experimentation. In addition, D'Angelo remained rooted in a racially black orientation, whereas Prince often placed himself alongside white women in his music videos. There are no white women in D'Angelo's videos. For example, in the video for "Me and Those Dreamin' Eyes of Mine," D'Angelo makes eye contact with various women of color sitting in the nightclub, and in separate vignettes shares intimate and soft kisses with an attractive black woman. In this sense, D'Angelo's conventional heterosexual image was not the strongest contender as the rightful heir to Prince's throne. Arguably, in terms of style, Maxwell, another one-named artist, appeared as a more apt successor to Prince.

Unlike Prince and D'Angelo, who wrote, sung, and performed their own music, Maxwell was not a triple-threat artist. In contrast, and for the most part, Maxwell was a vocalist. Yet, due to his androgynous undertones, falsetto singing style, and sultry semiexotic sexual aura, he easily invited comparisons to Prince. These "Prince" elements best coalesced on his debut release *Urban Hang Suite* (1996) and the video for the track ". . . Till the Cops Come Knockin'." The song and video established Maxwell as a bona fide heartthrob and slow jam maestro. Maxwell also offered a more bohemian and racially integrated image in his music videos than D'Angelo, but he was not as inclusive of whites as Prince. Either way, in my mind, Maxwell was more a 1990s' version of Marvin Gaye than any decade of Prince. Maxwell, like Gaye, exuded a calm sensuality and cadence of an experienced lover on all of his songs and music videos. In this sense, Maxwell's image was in stark contrast to Prince's perpetual aura of a sexual outlaw, and even when Prince shed his sex-junkie tag he still appeared on the verge of a relapse. Maxwell played it cool. Maybe too cool, a characteristic that came to light with his sophomore release *Embrya* (1998).

The *Embrya* album was filled with ambient ballads, and even the more up-tempo material sounded comparable to saccharin mood music. The easy-listening character of *Embrya* seemed out of sorts with Prince-styled dance grooves and innovative musicianship. As a consequence, Maxwell sounded, at his best, like the male analogue of Sade, a smooth jazz rendering of soulfully accented, midtempo grooves. At his worst, Maxwell sounded like the male analogue of Sade, a contrived and overproduced version of instrumental jazz music that provided a wonderful ambient soundtrack for loft dinner parties. Ultimately, D'Angelo's version of neo-soul music, more so than any other neo-soul artist, helped satisfy the nostalgic desire for Prince's more R&B oriented and overlooked material released in the early 1980s, a point underscored when D'Angelo remade the 1985 Prince B-side classic "She's Always in My Hair," for the *Scream 2* (1997) soundtrack.

Although neo-soul did revitalize black musicianship in the mid- to late 1990s, the genre suffered from its own excesses. Neo-soul was often either too idiosyncratic or prone to retreading previous R&B styles. Moreover, upon reflection, the overwhelming majority of neo-soul artists were a flash in the pan. Unlike Prince they were unable to sustain the level of creative genius first displayed in their genre-defining first releases. A retrospective plotting shows decreasing sales and relevancy for artists such as Erykah Badu, Lauryn Hill, Jill Scott, Musiq Soulchild, and Groove Theory, to name only a few. Possibly only Alicia Keys is the neo-soul artist able to demonstrate consistency over the long haul. Tellingly, she included a cover of Prince's bluesy lovers lament, "How Come You Don't Call Me Anymore," on her 2001 career-defining debut, *Songs in the Key of A Minor*. Regardless of the initial excitement concerning neo-soul or the tentative longevity of the genre, Prince had revolutionized black music multiple times, across nearly two decades, by the time neo-soul asserted its presence in the mid-1990s. Even Prince's hip-hop misfires of the 1990s would later prove prescient. In this regard, I find Prince's subsequent focus on hip-hop similar to Miles Davis's shift, in the early 1970s, from acoustic jazz to electric funk with his release, *On the Corner* (1972).

Because Davis viewed himself as disconnected from young African American music listeners, who had gravitated to the dance music of James Brown, Sly Stone, and the rock-blues of Jimi Hendrix, he consciously tried to create an album's worth of music that could connect with black youth. Consequently, *On the Corner* incorporated rhythm-heavy arrangements and groove-focused riffs with a repetitive drumming beat. For Stanley Crouch, a long-standing advocate and, at turns, vociferous critic of Davis, when Davis turned toward electric music it was a sonic betrayal of epic proportions, and *On the Corner* marks the apotheosis of Davis's musical blasphemy. According to Crouch, "Davis made much fine music for the first half of his professional life, and represented for many the uncompromising Afro-American artist contemptuous of Uncle Tom, but he has fallen from grace—and been celebrated for it. As usual, the fall from grace has been a form of success. Desperate to maintain his position at the forefront of modern music, to sustain his financial position, to be admired for the hipness of his purported innovations, Davis turned butt to the beautiful in order to genuflect before the commercial."[22] Crouch sounds more like a spurned lover than a sober music critic. From a more holistic perspective, Davis's music choice was informed as much by racial politics as by commercial demands. Most importantly, regardless of Crouch's disgruntled opinion, and like many of Miles Davis's prior forays into the sonic unknown, *On the Corner* prefigured a variety of musical styles and emergent musical trends. The album is a prototype of drum and bass, broken-beat music, and dub-step.[23]

Toward the end of his career and life Davis would again court critics' derision when he dropped his own hip-hop album, the posthumous *Do-Bop* (1992), that contained muted horn riffs mixed with beats created by Easy Mo Bee. At the time, the jazz–hip-hop hybrid garnered tepid reviews upon release and seemed dated. Yet *Do-Bop* was in tune with the growing popularity of the acid jazz meets hip-hop mash-up musical movement that emerged from the underground London club scene in the late 1980s and early 1990s, a sound best epitomized by the British group Soul II Soul. The aural ambiance of *Do-Bop* later returned as trip-hop and down-tempo grooves, all soundscapes that fused hip-hop beats with jazz instrumentation. Similarly, Prince was just like Miles Davis, when he experienced derision by critics and fans for trying to absorb hip-hop into his musical lexicon.

When Prince merged his "Minneapolis sound" with emergent hip-hop musical styles, it invited Prince purists (like myself) and hip-hop purists (like myself) to view Prince as an opportunist rather than an innovator. In fact, Prince's blending of hip-hop with his own sonic proclivities foretold of musical styles to come regarding hip-hop. For instance, the track "Sexy M.F." combined an exceptional R&B hook with mediocre rapping and prefigured what Sean "Puffy" Combs accomplished as a hit-making producer, a style epitomized on Mase's *Harlem World* (1997) release. Prince's semisuccessful blend of R&B with hip-hop experimentation was later perfected with artists like Kanye West and Drake on their respective releases *Late Registration* (2005) and *View* (2016). The result was sonic ear candy that made for radio-friendly hits and dance club bangers that moved the crowd. As Ahmir "Questlove" Thompson has rightfully noted, Prince was a hip-hop forerunner.[24]

Unfortunately, irrespective of Prince's creative foresight, he released a deluge of junk albums and weird music heading into the new millennium. *Emancipation* (1996) was a bloated three-disc CD set containing thirty-six unmemorable songs. The similarly situated *Crystal Ball* (1998) release comprised thirty demo-sounding odds and ends, a theme repeated with the throwaway tracks assembled on *The Vault: Old Friends 4 Sale* (1999). Before the new millennium "The Artist" dropped his twenty-third studio album, *Rave Un2 the Joy Fantastic* (1999), a CD crammed with a hodgepodge of guest performers. On the verge of the new millennium, Prince had become The Kid from *Purple Rain*, and the dialogue between his character and Billy, the club owner, in the film seemed eerily prophetic.

> BILLY: This stage is no place for your personal shit, man!
> THE KID: That's life, man.
> BILLY: Life, my ass, motherfucker! This is a business, and you ain't too far gone to see that yet! I told you before, you're not packin' them in like you used to. . . . No one digs your music but yourself.

This is not to say no one bought Prince's late-1990s material. Rather the material was made regardless of any forethought concerning its quality for a potential audience. It was Prince doing his own musical thing, but by the end of 1999 it appeared he was, oops, out of time.

When Prince changed his name to an unpronounceable glyph and became "symbol man," in a quest to conquer Warner Bros. Records, the various transformations Prince had made over several decades reached their nadir. Arguably, however, Prince was not the Artist Formerly Known as Prince to black folk. Supposedly, he let black people call him Prince during this period, a sensibility that suggested Prince was not estranged from "blackness."[25] He was just strange. It would take *Chappelle's Show* (2003–2004), a wildly successful sketch comedy series that trafficked almost exclusively in racially charged material, to remind the public that Prince was not just a peculiar figure clad in purple but a captivating black weirdo.

Chappelle's Show premiered on the cable network channel Comedy Central. Dave Chappelle was the host and creative cornerstone of the TV series, and the show quickly proved a programming surprise, earning the praise of fans and critics. The show was often praised for lampooning racial stereotypes and the intelligent use of racial irony, and, at times, Chappelle was sidesplittingly funny. For me, however, the show had a tendency to lean more toward the sophomoric than the satiric, and Chappelle's absurdist aesthetic rarely went beyond silly characterizations of black folk alongside cardboard representations of whites. For example, Chappelle and his cast constructed a race reversal parody of the MTV reality show *The Real World* (1992–2013). The sketch places Chad, a naive and hapless young white man, in a New York loft apartment with several black roommates. All the black roommates are hostile, many are drug users, and one is a sexual terrorist. A black roommate cuckolds Chad when his white girlfriend visits him. Later, they stab Chad with a sharp object in the apartment like it was a prison yard hit. I'm confident Chappelle intended to lampoon the racial politics of MTV that chaffed Rick James's career and which Prince creatively circumvented. Unfortunately, the MTV sketch also extolled the pathology of African Americans as irrational, violent criminals that prey on unsuspecting and innocent whites.

Eventually, at the height of his commercial popularity and executive power, Chappelle's rendering of black caricatures caught up with him. Chappelle became insecure about the type of black racial representation he presented to the public and abruptly stopped performing, walked off the set, and never returned.[26] The "show" was over. Despite the limitations and brevity of Chappelle's brand of comedic race baiting, for a brief but intense moment Chappelle aptly fulfilled the role of a keen arbiter of taste in black popular culture. In particular, Chappelle demonstrated his hipness quotient by featuring musical performances of premier black hip-hop and neo-soul artists on his show and delivering various skits that contained flashes of comic brilliance. Case in point, Chappelle's droll reenactment of an impromptu "real-life" basketball game between Prince and Eddie Murphy was not only humorous it also asserted how Prince was fluent in the cultural signifiers of blackness.

The sketch begins as a "True Hollywood" mock documentary with Chappelle playing Prince at a party.[27] Out of boredom Prince invites Murphy and company over to his home to shoot hoops. Once there, Prince challenges Murphy's crew to compete against him and his band in a basketball game, a contest Charlie Murphy narrates as "shirts against blouses." Chappelle's version of Prince mugs for the camera and plays basketball in attire similar to what Prince wore in the climactic concert performance in the film *Purple Rain*. The sketch ends with Prince reverse dunking the basketball and asserting his court dominance by declaring Murphy and his teammates are "bitches." Later Prince makes nice by serving pancakes to the losers of the game.

Chappelle's take on Prince, as a loveable weirdo, was a keen performance that grew in popularity, a point underscored a decade later when Prince used a still picture of Chappelle holding a silver platter full of pancakes dressed as him for the artwork tied to his song "Breakfast Can Wait" (2013). Most importantly, by Chappelle incorporating and exaggerating the peculiar mannerisms and personality ticks associated with Prince he promoted the weirdness of Prince as a source of entertainment in and of itself. As Chappelle, according to the dictates of Charlie Murphy as eyewitness storyteller, shoots hoops and trash talks his opponents dressed as Prince, he symbolically proxies and vouches for Prince as a black man. In this sense, "Prince's 'Blackness'—both his skills on the court as well as his flamboyant stage persona—is thus given cultural credibility by Murphy's story."[28] Accordingly, Prince's "blackness" in the Chappelle skit succeeds in undermining the image of Prince as alienated from contemporary black culture as well as affirming how his eccentricity is fused with his cultural blackness. The skit also poked holes in the Prince "cult-artist" persona while simultaneously embracing it, a feat that, ultimately, served to humanize Prince as a cool black weirdo for a generation of millennials to rediscover. But how far would they go back and what version of Prince would they claim?

Early in his career Prince was situated between R&B styles (e.g., Earth, Wind and Fire) on one side, and niche underground black funk groups (e.g., Parliament) on the other. Prince's alternative sexual expressivities were a subversive ploy to break out of this R&B polarity and subvert the narrow racial expectations and categories placed on black musicians and their music through fluid gender construction, insurgent style, sexual subtext, and flamboyant sexual prose. Prince's androgyny, sexual appetite, and willingness to explore taboo sexual desire and kink created an instant calling card of controversy that halted his being typecast as just another sexy, soul R&B performer. The mid-1990s marked a surprising about-face with Prince clearly invested in black popular culture vis-à-vis hip-hop music. At the end of the 1990s, all this shape-shifting proved a double-edged sword for Prince. Sure Prince proved he was highly adaptable to a shifting racial, cultural, and sonic landscape, but he lost his footing several times and his missteps were conveyed in the quality of the material he was putting out.

In the final analysis, for the first decade of Prince's career he played a game of racial hide-and-seek and constructed elaborate ruses to create distinct musical styles, one white and focused on pop crossover success and the other attuned to a black aural palate of slow jams and funky dance grooves. Much of the second decade of Prince's career was spent aping the vernacular and mechanics of hip-hop. Across both phases of his creative output Prince maintained his status as a sexual outlaw. By 2000 Prince's purple freak flag was well worn, and he was in need of a different banner. The following year, Prince abandoned his sex jones lyrics of the past, turned away from the profane, and embraced the sacred. Like a variety of legendary black recording artists who built careers on sexualizing their music then "saw the light," Prince got religion.

6

Don't Call It a Comeback . . .

We had to give up a lot for them [contemporary black entertainers] *to have what they have. I had to wait 40 minutes for my grits. This generation gets their grits in five minutes.*
—Paul Mooney, Comic Genius

At first glance, Prince's shift to a sanctified lifestyle appeared dramatic. In fact, when Prince redirected his life toward a faith-based orientation he joined the ranks of an assortment of black musicians who became religious, often later in their life and professional career. For example, music industry legends such as Little Richard, Al Green, and Donna Summer moved away from the secular music world and became faith-based artists. Some even took their change of heart as a "calling" and became ministers, like former soul man Al Green, and a slew of rappers, such as MC Hammer (Stanley Burrell), Mase (Mason Betha), Speech (Todd Thomas) of the defunct rap group Arrested Development, and Joseph Simmons, the first half of the groundbreaking rap group Run-DMC. For me, the most interesting aspect of any entertainer's religious conversion is not what is affirmed in the wake of a religious transformation and the lifestyle renounced but what type of career success freshly minted faith-based artists go on to achieve. Given that the line between secular fan and religious follower is a thin one, in many ways, taking on the mantle of a minister is less of a disavowal of their past career as a celebrity and more of a continuation of their secular star persona in a different context. In this sense, the turn toward religion for former entertainers can both provide a platform for a new lease on life and fuel a second and third act for a career stuck in the doldrums.

On the one hand, the best example of a successful black music artist able to merge the sacred and the popular at the peak of his career is Stevie Wonder. Wonder's ascendant phase as an artist and the popularity of his music dovetailed with the heightened interests in Eastern philosophy and various liberatory impulses of the late 1960s and early 1970s circulating in America. In particular, the decade of the 1970s gave birth to New Age humanism, with its talk of "vibes," meditation practice, and speculation concerning reincarnation.[1] Wonder's "golden" period perfectly synthesized the spirit of the time with his spiritual sensibility and the sonic pageantry conjured up on his Moog keyboard synthesizer. The cumulative result was elegantly expressed with sumptuous melodies on several successive releases: *Music of My Mind* (1972), *Talking Book* (1972), *Innervisions* (1973), *Fulfillingness' First Finale* (1974), and the magna opus *Songs in the Key of Life* (1976) and concluded with the curious experimental release, *Stevie Wonder's Journey through "The Secret Life of Plants"* (1979). For Wonder, gaining a high degree of creative freedom from his Motown label enabled him to assert a more spiritually and self-reflective lyrical content, a point of view that grew even more intense after his near fatal car accident.[2]

On the other hand, Richard Penniman (aka Little Richard) is an excellent example of an artist that renounced his secular career at the apex of his popularity for a church ministry. In the 1950s, Little Richard's flamboyant stage persona thrilled as well as startled white audiences with his showmanship and string of hit singles until he decided to abandon his career and pursue a new calling as a gospel singer. After releasing a handful of faith-based recordings Richard disappeared into relative obscurity for several decades until he took a bit role in the film *Down and Out in Beverly Hills* (1986). Richard played the part of Orvis Goodnight, a record producer and sole black resident in Beverly Hills, California. This new round of exposure revitalized Richard's career and garnered him appearances in a multitude of television shows. He even enjoyed modest success with the release of the song "Great Gosh A'mighty (It's a Matter of Time)," a gospel-styled and lyrical version of Richard's boogie-woogie classic "Good Golly Miss Molly."

In contrast to Wonder and Richard, Prince embraced the Jehovah's Witness sect of Christianity during the downward portion of his professional recording career.[3] This observation is not meant to suggest his conversion was disingenuous or a cynical personal choice of a man down on his luck in life. Not at all. Prince had explored religious themes at the height of his popularity and mastery of the musical moment. For example, on the B-side of the "Purple Rain" single is the song "God." Although a well-intentioned track, the Prince penned and performed song is overwrought with overdubs and an example of underwhelming sermonizing. Even with the *Lovesexy* release, which provided a more accessible style and sonic framework to express his spiritual sensibility, Prince's take on merging the popular with the nonsecular was bland. Unlike Wonder, Prince's attempts at overt spiritual songs were more strained than reflective and more reserved than uplifting, a sentiment underscored by the quiet storm jazz-fusion music on *The Rainbow Children* (2001) release. Given that Prince's career was built off of songs advocating freaky sex and included proclamations about doing "twenty-three positions in a one night stand," the upshot of the matter was what type of career success Prince could achieve as a black faith-based artist.

For Prince, a spiritually centered life as a Jehovah's Witness meant retooling his image more than remaking his music. Accordingly, the most pressing aspect of Prince's faith-based makeover was retiring his sex junkie past for a suave romantic figure. This G-rated, benign, and family-friendly Prince was already in the making. Prince previewed this middle-of-the-road image on the video for his top ten hit single, "The Most Beautiful Girl in the World" (1994). The video shows Prince showcasing a sexual politics of sensuous praise and appreciation of womanhood, female accomplishment, marriage, and family. "The Most Beautiful Girl in the World" video was a harbinger of the "grown and sexy" sensibility Prince adopted from the mid-2000s forward and fully formed on his comeback album *Musicology* (2004). *Musicology* reached #3 on the *Billboard* music chart, garnered two Grammy awards for Prince in the best R&B vocalist categories, and signaled that Prince was officially "old school."

"Old school," is a phrase used in African American culture to denote respect and appreciation to a previous style or way of being and doing. The

"Musicology" video clearly indicated that Prince was about the old school. The video showed two black men trying to enter a club venue wearing gold chains and jogging suits, a clichéd rendering of hip-hop style. They are repeatedly rebuffed by a security guard and barred from entering the club. Next, a well-dressed entourage strolls past the two men and is granted immediate access. The scene is evocative of Jay-Z's edict to "Change Clothes," a song from his *The Black Album* (2003), whereby the renowned rapper admonished Hip-Hop Nation to retire the baggy clothes for more mature, sophisticated, and fashion-forward attire. In "Musicology" Prince advocates the same sensibility. Prince's promotion of an old school sensibility should not surprise anyone. By 2008 Prince had been recording and performing for thirty years and was fifty years old. How could anyone expect a perpetual shape-shifter to remain fixed in time singing about getting fellatio and giving cunnilingus on the sly? Prince's change in direction did not define Prince as a sexual hypocrite. Within the framework of his newfound religious belief Prince still dabbled in the erotic, but vulgarity was no longer part of Prince's image or music. Ironically, in contrast to his trench coat sexual outlaw image of the past, this "plain" and chaste version of Prince was also a radical figure. Not only was the new Prince a break from the old Prince it was a disruptive presence in black music—again.

For a generation of American kids born in the early 1990s and coming of age in the new millennium, sex and graphic displays of the human body were passé. In the wake of a rap group like N.W.A., which detailed their misogynistic exploits and brutally graphic takedown of a young woman on the track "She Swallowed It," off the *Niggaz4Life* (1991) release, the shock factor of Prince singing about a woman that enjoyed masturbation in a public lobby was lightweight fare. Not surprisingly, a decade later hip-hop music openly flirted with the commercial viability of pornography as an aesthetic perspective and practice.[4] For example, *BET: Uncut* (2001–2006), a late night cable TV show, presented nearly X-rated rap videos on TV and made a name for itself with Nelly's "Tip Drill Remix" (2003), a video that had Nelly swipe a credit card between a black woman's nearly naked buttocks. With videos like this it became evident that hip-hop presented black female bodies as objects of bacchanalian revelry and black porn was going mainstream. In addition, the abundant presence of and easy access to Internet pornography of the 2000s marked how American society was steadily transforming into the pornotopia Daniel Bell predicted in his book *The Cultural Contradictions of Capitalism* (1976). Against this backdrop, the soft-core peekaboo sexual optics and lyrical tendencies Prince deployed for much of his own career were dated.

Ironically, Prince's turn to the sacred and embrace of a sexually conservative stance reaffirmed Prince's against-the-grain sensibility for a public accustomed to his sexualized persona. For others who were more intimately involved with Prince in the past he was way behind the curve. Several former members of his musical entourage had already rejected and retreated from the hypersexual and hedonistic image Prince had fashioned years before Prince made his religious transformation.[5] Gayle Chapman bailed earliest. She was the keyboard player for Prince's first touring band until 1980 and went on to explore Christian-focused music. In 1983, Dez Dickerson left Prince's band due to the raunchy content of Prince's material; he felt it was at odds with his growing Christian beliefs. Several years later, after a near-death experience in the late 1990s, Denise Matthews (aka Vanity) found faith and disavowed her Prince-created persona.

Religious conversion for Prince was not as draconian as that of his former bandmates. Prince adopted a more flexible sexual sensibility and included just enough romantic eroticism to maintain an air of vulnerability and daring, a style epitomized on the music videos for the songs "Te Amo Corazón" and "Black Sweat" off the *3121* (2006) studio album. Additionally, Prince's religious conversion did not impede his commercial drive to create and distribute new music. In the mid-2000s, Prince was releasing new music at an accelerated clip, a majority of it as digital downloads for members of his website, and simply giving away numerous copies of his studio-released CDs.

For instance, concertgoers for the *Musicology* tour got the *Musicology* release with their ticket purchases. In England, the *Planet Earth* (2007) release was included for free with the Sunday paper edition of the *Mail on Sunday*. As Prince grew increasingly comfortable playing his back catalog these promotional gimmicks were less about his current music releases and more geared toward driving awareness for Prince concerts.[6] In due course, this shift in marketing and distribution marked how Prince was becoming less known for pumping out new chart-dominating hits and increasingly valued as a live performer and entertainer extraordinaire. For more than two decades Prince had churned out hit music. At this point, Prince fans did not necessarily want to purchase his new studio releases, they just wanted to see Prince perform. Fittingly, in 2006, Prince took up residency in Las Vegas, as a headliner act.

On the one hand, Las Vegas is considered a destination for washed-up pop stars past their prime scrounging up paychecks as lounge acts for middle-aged tourist types. If Elvis Presley is the benchmark for this career cliché then such a strident observation is true. Elvis Presley, one of the most celebrated cultural icons in American pop culture, ended his career in Las Vegas, a shell of his former self. On the other hand, resting in the center of Presley's downward spiral is the fact that only a significant entertainer can headline in Sin City. To this point, Presley remains the paradigmatic entertainer as a renowned recording artist and hit film star with record sales in the hundreds of millions. Prince was similarly situated as Presley. Prince was a legendary entertainer, celebrated recording artist, and hit film star with record sales over a hundred million. Such statistics put Prince in the rare echelon of a pop icon that possessed the requisite years of longevity, name notoriety, accomplishment, and musical influence, a figure fitting the status of a headlining Vegas act.

Prince put his headliner status to the test twice a week for six months at the Rio Hotel and Casino. The results? A local Las Vegas weekly paper declared Prince's Vegas run so successful it was ranked number 12 on a top 25 all-time headliner lists.[7] Admittedly, Prince's extended stint in Vegas suggested the twilight of a major entertainer's career. In fact, it was the beginning of Prince's third act in his nearly four-decade career and further cemented his status as a compelling mainstream crossover artist. Prince had come an astounding distance from being booed off the stage at the LA Coliseum. Then he was a black man trying to play white rock music to please a rowdy and overwhelmingly white rock crowd. Now he just played his music, and that was enough to draw adoring fans of all races.

For the most part, during the 1980s, Prince was trying to make you forget he was black. Somewhere in the middle of the 1990s Prince tried proving how black he was. In the 2000s, it appeared American mainstream pop culture was willing to forget Prince was black at all. For example, Prince was no longer a controversial headlining choice for a predominantly white rock event. Take his 2004 guest performance to posthumously induct George Harrison into the Rock and Roll Hall of Fame. Prince joined legendary white rock musicians Tom Petty, Jeff Lynne, and Steve Winwood onstage and played the lead guitar solo at the end of the Beatles song "While My Guitar Gently Weeps" (1968). What reservations may have existed prior to Prince's striking his first guitar lick evaporated in a virtuoso solo performance that upstaged everyone on stage. The Rock and Roll Hall of Fame performance demonstrated, in the most basic of optics, that Prince's career was one of not merely breaking through racial barriers in the recording industry but shattering obstructions.

Prince's run of high-profile mainstream gigs continued in 2007 with an electrifying half-time show for Super Bowl XLI. Prince was a provocative pick in the post–Janet Jackson era of half-time Super Bowl shows. In 2004, Jackson and Justin Timberlake were performing onstage and Timberlake pulled off a part of Jackson's wardrobe to correspond to a line in the song declaring how he wanted her naked. To the audience's surprise a portion of the costume was removed and exposed her right breast nipple. The peekaboo nipple stunt shocked millions of unsuspecting viewers and stirred a public uproar over indecency in America. Timberlake, as a white male, ripping the clothes off a black woman, seemingly against her will and to her utter surprise, evoked centuries-old issues concerning sexual imposition by white men on black women's bodies going back to American slavery. Against this cultural backdrop, Prince took to the stage and put to shame the sexual hijinks of Jackson and Timberlake with a legendary performance. Fully clothed, wearing a teal suit and matching suede boots, paired with a bright orange shirt, Prince was able to pull off a more shocking and entertaining spectacle than Jackson and Timberlake with their trite attempt at partial nudity.

During a deluge of rain Prince performed a medley of hit songs from other rock acts, sprinkled in a few of his own, then closed out the rain-filled event with his signature song, "Purple Rain." When he begins his guitar solo a gigantic billowing silk-screen-like scrim, illuminated from below, unfurled from the stage and created a giant silhouette of Prince playing his guitar. Even after multiple viewings of Prince holding center stage by himself I'm still struck by the image of him standing behind the enormous fluttering scrim, holding his symbol guitar between his legs, and playing a Jimi Hendrix–style guitar solo. The silhouette made Prince appear like a colossal satyr, a sex demigod, with a monstrous erect penis pointing to the sky. Undoubtedly, his performance is ripe for deconstructing the sexual politics of the male black body, particularly concerning the size of black men's genitals as a site of white anxieties and fantasy projection.[8] Ultimately, however, the imagery is most reflective of Prince finding a way to bring his unique brand of sexual flamboyance to the half-time Super Bowl show on his own terms. Vintage Prince.

The half-time show for Super Bowl XLI is an excellent example of how the spectacle of Prince, as an entertainer, effortlessly overshadowed any particular racial discourse or stigma concerning Prince as a stereotypical articulation of a hypersexualized black man. Admittedly, much of the first part of Prince's career was overtly committed to eluding categorization by a music-marketing industrial complex intent on labeling and containing black music. In response, Prince fashioned exotic identities. His most brazen effort was when Prince constructed a false narrative around having a white parent, a point Touré deconstructs in his book *I Would Die 4 U*. Touré views Prince's claims of having a white parent as a ploy to maneuver around conventional racism.

Touré goes on, at length, to deploy the term "passing" as a point of reference and explain how Prince used it as a racial tactic to gain material advantages:

> Passing, historically, is about effectively becoming white. To this point, some African Americans took advantage of their light skin pigmentation and "white like appearance and escaped to an area where no one knew their family and their past so they could be perceived as white and live as if they were white. Passing is not about hating Blackness but about giving yourself the best possible chance in life. It's about refusing to allow white supremacy's harsh judgment of Black potential to constrain your life's journey. It's about fooling the society that would punish Blackness and exploiting a loophole in the system.⁹"

Touré gets the general racial topography correct but his racial map is incomplete in accurately accounting for how the racial landscape is gerrymandered. Racial passing, as it applies to Prince, only makes sense if Prince was trying to "fool" people, make them believe he was white. But anyone that has ever seen a picture of Prince readily recognizes that he is not a white man. Touré chooses to conflate racial passing with passing as a mixed-raced person without explaining what "mixed-raced person" means and what advantages are attached to such a status.

Prince's false construction of having a white parent speaks to a tactic used by black folk to increase their social prestige and cultural capital in white America by creating an exotic racial identity. Louis Chude-Sokei in his book *The Last "Darky": Bert Williams, Black-on-Black Minstrelsy, and the African Diaspora* (2006) makes this marvelous observation concerning black folk falsifying and manufacturing their ethic background as a racial masquerade done for increased prestige: "This masquerade was also a common practice . . . among black con men and hucksters. For them, the exotic authenticity of the African mask enabled a greater degree of social mobility than plain old despised black skin. In *Pan-Africanism from Within*, Ras Makonnen describes how this intra-racial passing/masquerade could work against racism in America: 'Once you had discovered this American folly, you would put on your fez and "pass" like any other white. . . . People might think you were an African prince.'"[10]

When Prince claimed he was a mulatto, racially mixed, or, in the racial nomenclature of today, of biracial lineage, he created an exotic aura of racial difference. I assume Prince believed, in the eyes of the American music industry and the music-consuming public, that presenting a racial narrative where he is half white would grant him, at most, more latitude to play rock music. Perhaps even, at the least, permit Prince, during a Super Bowl halftime show, to symbolize a satyr with an outrageously huge erect penis and avoid the stigma of racial stereotypes and cultural consternation concerning the black body. Imagine if Jay-Z, Chris Brown, Fetty Wap, or Travis Scott had done the same thing.

A key weakness, however, of the "mixed raced" ploy is it invites criticism that pawning oneself off as half white, when you are not, can just as easily reflect a belief whiteness is a preferred and most socially desirable racial identity to have in America. Such a stance speaks more to black self-hatred and has little, to nothing, to do with some subversive music-marketing gambit to con the system. In the long run, I tack more toward Touré in framing the type of racial reconfiguration Prince engaged in as an "act" more than a personal insight concerning how Prince felt as an African American man. For me, the issue of racial "passing" with Prince is less about "passing" and more about creating an aura of ambiguous and exotic blackness as a strategic and subversive form of image creation. Such racial misdirection along with a brash sexuality, that bordered on farce, was necessary in order to effectively navigate the Jim Crow American music industry, the racial badlands of American pop culture, and the strident racial politics of the conservative Reagan era of the 1980s.

Generate enough contradictory meaning and you become increasingly difficult to define, are almost impossible to categorize, and appear perpetually defiant. This is early-1980s Prince; straight/gay, black/white, God fearing/atheist. As a consequence, Prince was not only an affront to mainstream morality but, for broader strategic purposes, made himself an unwieldy persona unable to fit into the standard musical minority categories allotted for black music artists during that period. This rebellious undercurrent was still palpable deep into Prince's career. Just check Prince's pre–Super Bowl XLI press conference. Prince and his band enter the room, and, instead of answering questions, he performed an impromptu rocked-out version of "Anotherloverholenyohead," a track from the *Parade* release. Then there is Prince's disregard for stage protocol among his white musician peers at the Rock and Roll Hall of Fame to posthumously induct George Harrison. At the end of his guitar solo he removes his guitar, nonchalantly tosses it up in the air, his point person, ensconced in the audience near the raised platform, catches it, and Prince struts off the stage while the other lead white musicians remain there to bring the song to a close. On the one hand, Prince's disregard for stage protocol smacks of arrogance. On the other hand, his stunt is open for interpretation as a move that is not merely an expression of overbearing showmanship but a tactic taken straight from the Miles Davis book of black insolent cool.[11]

Davis was known to perform with his back to the audience and made a racial qualification between confidence and arrogance: white people, he said, get confidence mixed up with arrogance. If people of any color other than white are confident, they are called arrogant.[12] Prince's solo performance at the posthumous induction of George Harrison at the Rock and Roll Hall of Fame underscored his subversive agency articulated at the beginning of his music profession and throughout his career, a defiance born of operating in a very racially constrained music industry. In this sense, even the tone-deaf symbolism of having the word "Slave," scrawled on his cheek clearly demonstrated how issues concerning race, power, and personal identity were perpetually churning just below the surface of Prince's mysterious and often impenetrable persona. In the wake of the election of an African American man, Barack Obama, as president of the Unite States, Prince's racial dissuasions would rise further to the surface.

In the heady afterglow of America's first black president and a black first family in the White House, the role of race dictating the success or failure of individual African Americans seemed retrograde in comparison to the symbolic promise Obama represented. The American body politic appeared ready to make good on Prince's racial yearning expressed on "Controversy" when he said, "I wish there was no black or white." Obama was president because a significant number of white voters had chosen him as the best candidate for the office, a clear indication that in America it was not about black or white. Or was it?

A groundswell of public concern, outrage, and national attention was generated around race in the wake of the fatal shooting of Trayvon Martin, an unarmed seventeen-year-old African American high school student, by a neighborhood watch volunteer in 2012, a spate of black fatalities during encounters with law enforcement, and a surging black-on-black murder rate in Chicago. The progressive racial symbolism of Obama's presidency gave way to an on-the-ground racial reality of increasing racial friction and social disillusionment concerning American race relations. Prince tentatively entered the fray to address this trend by teaming up with Van Jones, a former special adviser in the Obama administration concerning environmental equality, and committed to performing three benefit concerts set over three evenings in Chicago for Jones's Rebuild the Dream organization. Prince promoted the benefit concert by appearing on *The View* (1997–present), a female-hosted television talk show that examines a variety of current events and topics. Prince strutted on stage sporting what is referred to colloquially in African American nomenclature as a baby Afro.

For thirty-three years, Prince wore some form of a chemically relaxed hairstyle. Accordingly, for Prince to break from having a chemically treated hairstyle was more than just a stylistic point of departure; it situated Prince in a broader, ongoing, and pitched racial discussion concerning American race relations and black racial identity. In the past, a black person's hairstyle signified a series of political implications and cultural affirmations. In *The Autobiography of Malcolm X* (1965), Malcolm X lamented how, as a young man, he chemically straightened his hair to look white and later deemed it an act of racial self-degradation and self-mutilation. Soon after, as the Black Power movement gained momentum in the mid- to late 1960s, a new hairstyle emerged to symbolize their radical racial pride—the Afro.

By the late 1960s even James Brown, a black entertainer known for his "processed" hairstyle, had gone natural to promote racial pride. When James Brown, decades earlier, stopped chemically straightening his hair to don an Afro hairstyle it signified an increasingly overt level of political expressiveness. Similarly, Prince's drastic style transformation was not detached from social context. Just three years earlier, Solange Knowles had shaved her chemically relaxed tresses for a natural hairstyle, a personal style choice that animated Twitter debates and became a public flashpoint around a "natural hair movement." In this regard, Prince's return to a natural hairstyle was part and parcel of a new generation of bohemian African Americans and their advocacy of organic hairstyles and the racial politics they signified.

Even though Prince episodically expressed his political awareness in the past with songs such as "Ronnie Talk to Russia," "Free," "Sign o' the Times," and "Cinnamon Girl," Prince's attempt at political relevancy most often appeared casual and ephemeral. Such as when, in 1985, at the pinnacle of his popularity, Prince donated the track "4 the Tears in Your Eyes," to go on the *We Are the World* (1985) album instead of participating alongside a variety of famous and accomplished recording artists invited to sing "We Are the World," a song dedicated to raise money for Ethiopian famine relief. Ridicule and public scorn soon followed Prince.[13] *Saturday Night Live* comic Billy Crystal dressed up as Prince for a skit that included Hulk Hogan and Mr. T acting as bodyguards. The skit presented Prince as completely self-absorbed by having his bodyguards fend off other music stars that tried to sing into his microphone. Thirty years would pass before Prince fully shed the self-absorbed pop-cult figure of his "We Are the World" past. At the 57th annual Grammy awards Prince stated, "Albums, like books and black lives, still matter, tonight and always." During his *Purple Rain* heyday it was virtually unthinkable that Prince would assert any public acknowledgment concerning black politics.

The point of the matter is that Prince was now publically asserting a black political identity informed by and expressed as cultural resistance and social advocacy for racial justice. He was no longer just a figure of nostalgic awe or a reclusive celebrity with a disconnected lifestyle from the black public. In particular, Prince's public support of the Black Lives Matter movement, an organization that drew a generous amount of criticism from white conservatives, police, and police advocates for condemning and protesting police killings of black people, demonstrated Prince was squarely on the side of black protest. Moreover, Prince's comment at the Grammy awards show were just a preview of an intensifying embrace and meaningful advocacy of black racial politics.[14]

One of Prince's most conspicuous displays of a black political outlook and commitment to action arose in the aftermath of the funeral for Freddie Gray on April 27, 2015. Gray, a twenty-five-year-old African American man, incurred fatal injuries during his custody with Baltimore police officers. Moreover, Gray's death sparked community demonstrations and civil unrest following Gray's funeral. As demonstrations turned hostile with the burning of property, a state of emergency was declared in Baltimore, and National

Guard troops were promptly sent in to restore order. Against this dire back-drop Prince asserted his iconic presence and decided to hold a benefit concert in Baltimore called "Dance Rally 4 Peace," a few weeks later. Prince also encouraged concertgoers to wear the color gray, a symbolic tribute to the memory and meaning of Freddie Gray. The graphic design created to promote the "Dance Rally 4 Peace" concert displayed a mustachioed Prince wearing a gray turtleneck shirt with round sunglasses, sporting a large, perfectly round and proportioned Afro hairstyle. The look was clearly evocative of the stylized attire of black radicals and intellectuals during the late 1960s. The only item missing was a black leather jacket.

Prince also released "Baltimore," a protest song that contained confrontational lyrics drawing from the recent deaths of black men by white police officers in 2014, such as Michael Brown from Ferguson, St. Louis, and Eric Garner in New York City. The concert and protest song clearly demonstrated Prince making overt strides to inhabit the role of previous socially engaged black artists, as exemplified by Stevie Wonder's deep and long-standing commitment to racial justice, and make a track similar to Marvin Gaye's landmark protest song "What's Going On" (1971). "Baltimore" did not shoot up the charts as a hit song or even become the unofficial anthem for a social movement. In this regard, Prince was not a social voice like Curtis Mayfield, who created a number of songs during the 1960s that tapped into the black political aspirations of the Civil Rights movement and later provided the soundtrack for the urban undertow of postindustrial decline that plagued American black ghettos in the 1970s. Ultimately, Prince was not able to resonate as far and deep with "Baltimore" as had Wonder, Gaye, Mayfield, and subsequent artists, like Grandmaster Flash and the Furious Five with "The Message" (1982), Public Enemy with the protest anthem "Fight the Power" (1989), and, as of this writing, a significant portion of Kendrick Lamar's work on the album *To Pimp a Butterfly* (2015) along with Childish Gambino's (Donald Glover) music video for "This Is America" (2018).

Nonetheless, Prince's efforts around the civil unrest sparked by Gray's death reflected a profound concern with the state of black America, a point of concern revealed in the brief remarks around black self-determination and economic empowerment Prince made to the "Dance Rally 4 Peace" concert crowd in attendance. Prince told the audience, "The next time I come to Baltimore I want to stay in a hotel owned by you."[15] The "Dance Rally 4 Peace" concert marked an important milestone for Prince, not only with his outspoken identification with issues concerning racial justice but with his active intervention to quell violent social unrest. In this regard Prince's "Dance Rally 4 Peace" show is parallel to James Brown's free concert given in Boston, Massachusetts, the day after Dr. Martin Luther King Jr. was assassinated. Brown's concert is credited with dramatically quelling violent unrest in Boston.[16]

While Prince's racial politics evolved in a pattern of fits and starts his gender politics, though rife with contradictory impulses, continually defied conventional expectations. Admittedly, Prince cultivated and, in great measure, enacted various forms of sexual objectification with female performers, a point made most notably with the all-female group Vanity 6. Nevertheless, women have played a prominent role in much of Prince's career not merely as objects of voyeuristic scrutiny but as gainfully employed musicians in his various music projects. I can think of no solo artist of Prince's stature that promoted and presented women musicians as a part of his band or provided a space for their own solo career, starting with Gayle Chapman in Prince's first touring band and making the mixed-gender band a staple of his musical entourage.

Certainly, some of Prince's female "protégés," like Vanity (Denise Matthews) and Carmen Electra (Tera Patrick), evoke the image-controlling relationship found in Alfred Hitchcock's film *Vertigo* (1958), a psychological thriller where the male character's obsessions with assembling the appearance of his love interest defines the doomed nature of their relationship. Nevertheless, Prince was not merely using the music studio as a boudoir. As Prince achieved, managed, and mismanaged increasing levels of mainstream success across his career and massive body of musical output, he not only exhibited the rare ability to reinvent himself but also helped a variety of female musicians do the same. Accordingly, Prince produced a myriad of musical projects with formidable female musicians and songwriters, whether as former paramours, current protégés, or ongoing peers. Chaka Khan, Mavis Staples, Nona Hendryx, Sheena Easton, Susanna Hoffs of the Bangles, Wendy Melvion, Lisa Coleman, Sheila Escovedo, Taja Sevelle, and Rosie Gains demonstrate the depth of female talent Prince worked with in the studio and on stage.

In addition, Prince impacted a younger generation of black female musicians, a point underscored in 2010 at the BET Awards when Prince was honored by Afrofuturist hip-hop diva Janelle Monae with her cover of "Let's Go Crazy," followed by the extraordinary jazz bassist Esperanza Spalding singing "If I Was Your Girlfriend," along with pop pianist Alicia Keys performing "Adore." Even late in his career Prince still challenged conventional notions concerning gender in the music industry by pulling together an all-female touring band called 3rdEyeGirl. In the end, Prince showcased a variety of female talent; white women, black women, and mixed-race women who were super fit, superfine, overweight, blonde, brunette, and even bald. Consequently, over the course of Prince's nearly four-decade career he provided optics and opportunities for women to share their talent in a music industry prone to dismiss women as merely pliable groupies or eye candy for the male gaze.

In retrospect, Prince was at the vanguard of American popular culture and our collective imagination when making music and presenting various versions of himself for consumption, despite his frequently contradictory expressions and perceptions concerning the place of race, sexuality, and gender in the music industry. Moreover, not only was Prince at the forefront of reconfiguring our collective imagining of race, sexuality, and gender in popular music, he was one of the first major recording artists to recognize that the "wreka stow" was a construct firmly situated in the past. Throughout the 2000s and into the next decade, much of the new music Prince released was through nontraditional channels, such as promo-material, downloads, and streaming content via the Internet.

In particular, new Prince material was only available to members of Prince's music club website or music streaming service providers.[17] Today music is predominantly experienced as digital downloads from music streaming services. But when Prince used the Internet to distribute his music it was an example of his against-the-grain outlook and easily interpreted as another middle finger to the recording industry. Prince would eventually waiver from having the Internet as the sole provider and most viable distributer of his new material. Nonetheless, his commitment to online distribution of his music as the most accessible place to purchase his latest content was radical at the time.

Alongside Prince's rebellious sensibility he did periodically poke fun at himself and his status as a man of mystery, a pop icon shrouded in secrets. Case in point, Prince guest starred as himself on an episode of the network television sitcom *New Girl* (2014). The episode clearly capitalized on Prince's iconic superstar status to energize the flat comic punch lines and middling comedic chemistry between Jess (Zooey Deschanel) and her co-stars. In his guest-starring episode, Prince not only offers advice about love and life, he commands a butterfly to sit on his shoulder, delivers inside jokes about his penchant for pancakes, and ends the show with an auto-tuned duet performance with Jess and her co-stars dancing on stage. The show concludes with Jess's friends sitting in her apartment reflecting on their evening at Prince's mansion party. Jess closes with, "Prince is magic." Without a doubt, the episode celebrated and exemplified the eccentric wonder and cheerful flamboyance of Prince. The show is also historical. It marks one of the last television appearances of Prince before his premature passing.

As Prince's life force was ebbing he was busy creating new music and touring. Prince and his backing band, 3rdEyeGirl, did a bunch of gigs in Europe for Prince's Hit & Run tour during the spring and summer of 2014 before coming back stateside for a limited American tour in 2015. Then in the beginning of 2016, with his Piano & Microphone tour, Prince went in a radical direction that had him going back to basics. Prince occupied the stage alone, playing at the piano and singing songs. On April 14, 2016, Prince played a pair of Piano & Microphone shows in Atlanta, Georgia. Seven days later he died in an elevator at his Paisley Park estate.

7

Dearly Beloved

An Epitaph

> *Sometimes it snows in April*
> —Prince

During the mid-1980s the Oscar-nominated film *All That Jazz* (1979) would periodically get an uncut television showing on KCOP (Channel 13), a local television station in Los Angeles, California. Even though *All That Jazz* contained female frontal nudity and explicit language, the film was not edited for television. *All That Jazz* was considered to contain such a high degree of artistic merit that any editing, in any manner, would impair the meaning and value of the material (or so the argument went). In addition, as an independent station KCOP had more leeway with the type of programming presented and could test the threshold of public decency in a manner the big three national networks (ABC, CBS, and NBC) of the time could not. As a result, *All That Jazz* aired on KCOP uncut. The film was loosely based on Bob Fosse, a rich, successful, white Broadway musical theater choreographer. In multiple ways, the film's subject matter was extremely disconnected from my own life as a black teenager in a household headed by a single female, more working-poor than working-class. But given that I was a puberty-stricken adolescent with no cable television, the prospect of seeing an unedited R-rated film on regular television was quite appealing. I still vividly recall the film.

On first glance Sandahl Bergman's "hard body" appeal is likely anticipated as the reason I remember the film so well. Admittedly, Bergman displayed a kinetic eroticism during the "Take Off with Us" vignette where she pretended she was a flight stewardess. The number is an editing tour de force of quick cuts that transitions to a sensual chorus line of languorous semi-nude female and male bodies swaying together in orgiastic pantomimes, an erotic spectacle perfectly synced to a sumptuous acid-jazz soundtrack. Yet the vignette that has stayed with me the most over the years is the Lenny Bruce–inspired comic featured throughout the film. Peppered throughout *All That Jazz* is footage of Dave Newman (Cliff Gorman) repeatedly performing his standup material, riffing on the existential crisis of mortality. Newman tells his audience about, "This chick, man, without the benefit of dying herself, has broken down the process of dying into five stages: anger, denial, bargaining, depression and acceptance." The "chick" Newman keeps chastising in *All That Jazz* is Swiss American psychiatrist Elisabeth Kübler-Ross (1926–2004). She authored the groundbreaking book *On Death and Dying* (1969), a pioneering treatise that presented a five-stage model of grief.

The Kübler-Ross model is debatable for predicting sequential stages of behavior but after I received a text that Prince was dead, the multiple scenes of Newman performing his interpretation of those stages in *All That Jazz* haunted me for weeks. By the time I received news of his passing I had written most of my book on Prince and his strange relationship with race. Surprisingly, my emotional reactions to his death had very little to do with what impact his death may or may not have on my book project. Instead, my response seemed to mirror the Kübler-Ross model presented in the film *All That Jazz*. Certainly, "denial" was a dominant stage.

Even after I found the information of Prince's passing valid, it still took awhile for me to accept that one of my favorite youth-defining musicians had died. Moreover, as the musical tributes mounted, I was unable to take comfort in any of my favorite Prince material stored on my own iPhone, which primarily spanned the first half of his career from *For You* (1978) to *Sign o' the Times* (1987). For almost a year after Prince's death I did not listen to any of my personal collection of his past recordings. Instead, I binged on all the "new" music on the Internet, mostly demo versions of prior hits and bootleg concert material Prince was able to suppress when he was alive because of his aggressive and vigilant copyright surveillance of the Internet. Before I could listen to Prince, the man I musically adored, I had to come to terms with my anger at him.

I became increasingly angry as more details seeped into the public concerning his addiction to pain medicine, most likely exacerbated by a lifetime of high-intensity physical performances that demanded a high degree of athleticism executed in high-heeled boots. I was angry with Prince for believing his own press. For always being "Prince," the image, the icon, the larger-than-life figure that appeared not to age, the "Prince" of our/my youth. Prince stayed in character all the time, like Clayton Moore, the star of *The Lone Ranger* (1949–1957) television series, who persisted in wearing a mask in public decades after the show had ended. Moore had his mask. Prince had his high-heeled boots. Sure, at fifty-seven years old Prince still had the sullen doe-eyed look we remember from *Purple Rain*, but he was no longer the sauntering showman and limber dancer that could leap from a piano, land on the floor doing the splits, and pop up with ease. Prince still had the strut; the only difference was that he added a cane to round out the look. Personally, I thought the cane was just a prop and even with it Prince seemed to glide when he walked. In retrospect, given the powerful opioids he was consuming, to what degree Prince could feel his legs, knees, hips, ankles, and feet is debatable. How much more music made and time spent alive (and in less pain) if Prince had traded in his signature high-heeled style for a pair of Nikes or Adidas?

How amazing is the octogenarian country singer Willie Nelson, the Rolling Stones as a group, and Keith Richards as a man over seventy years old, for letting it all hang out (but still hanging in) playing gigs and making music during their advanced years? As it stands, Prince was addicted to pain relief prescriptions that aided in maintaining the illusion that Prince was still the same when he was not. It was depressing to discover that the unique and one-of-a-kind Prince would succumb to such a cliché, a pop star's demise due to drug dependency, drug abuse, and a drug overdose. Pop star addiction reeks of banality. Amy Winehouse made sure of that when she turned drug and alcohol dependency into a hit song entitled "Rehab," off her *Back to Black* (2006) studio release. The song included a catchy refrain to the proposition of drug rehabilitation, "I said no, no, no." Winehouse turned addiction into a popular little ditty with her irreverent refrain, then died five years later ravaged by drug and alcohol abuse. She was twenty-seven years old. Death by drug overdose is such a generic occurrence for musicians; a

Wikipedia page is devoted to listing pop musicians who have died of a drug overdose. It is a long list, and, as of this writing, Prince was the last name recorded but most likely will not be the last.

I have accepted the fact that Prince is gone. Yet the body of Prince's music remains an extensive presence. The outpouring of adoration given to Prince in the weeks, months, and years after his death demonstrates the broad impact, depth, and stature of his sprawling discography, recorded concert material, style, and image in the lives, hearts, and memories of millions of people around the world. Admittedly, the collective appreciation of his music and collective memory of the man are fractionalized. With Prince, when trying to define the type of music Prince created, where one musical genre begins and ends is rife with ambiguous and artificial dividing lines. Moreover, the broad appeal of Prince and his expansive musical output makes it all the more difficult for one group to claim Prince as their own or place him in one particular category. For example, is Prince an American music icon or one of America's greatest black superstars?

In the wake of Prince's premature passing the first wave of major music industry commemorations exposed the racial fault lines resting right below the surface of Prince's widespread crossover popularity. In particular, a contingent of fans voiced apprehension that a white woman, pop diva Madonna, was slated to perform a tribute to Prince at the 2016 Billboard Music awards and started an online petition to protest her as a headliner.[1] Soon after Madonna's tepid performance, Black Entertainment Television ran a commercial blurb as a teaser for their upcoming 2016 BET awards show set to pay tribute to Prince that read: "Yeah, we saw that. Don't worry. We got you."

The mocking tone of BET was ostensibly directed toward Madonna and Billboard Music, a white institutional publication arm of the recording industry. Beneath BET's sly signifying comments rested a deeper, historical, and ongoing racial critique. Keep in mind that BET emerged as a corrective for the exclusion of black music videos and black artists from MTV. Moreover, the BET award show was intended to give proper recognition to black artists that are often snubbed by white mainstream awards shows when they hand out official accolades. Consequently, the BET tribute to Prince functioned as a "corrective" to a white definition of Prince's place in America's collective imagination. Even in his passing Prince evoked long-standing racial politics and tensions in American popular culture and the American recording industry. Ultimately, in order to draw any real meaning from

Prince's life and legacy, it requires not just a deep memorization of his discography or praise for his musical innovations but also a critical contextualization of Prince's accomplishments against the racial environment he emerged from and operated in.

For starters, the American music industry operated in terms of a stringent, yet informal, racial code that governed how black and white recording artists were categorized and marketed. As a consequence, the recording industry was a decisive arbiter of musical taste, dictating along strict racial lines what was appropriate for music audiences to hear and purchase, similar to the Hollywood Motion Picture Production Code of the 1930s, commonly referred to as the Hays Code.

The Hays Code tried to enforce various cultural values concerning morality, crime, religion, and sexuality and dictated suitable content for audiences to consume. Similarly, during the mid-1970s to the late 1980s the American music industry enforced an informal racial code aimed at and concerned with appeasing album-oriented rock audiences. Moreover, the broader cultural politics of race in America articulated deep-seated racial anxieties through coded language. Richard Nixon's "southern strategy," of the late 1960s came to a head with the Reagan–Bush era white racial backlash of the 1980s, whereby deep-seated racial angst was used to appeal to white voters for political support and masked as "generic issues" threatening the civic well-being of the nation.[2] This neoconservative tactic gained traction not only in the realm of politics but across the entertainment landscape of American popular culture as ideologically coded material concerning race.

For instance, the 1980s delivered audiences films like *The Toy* (1982), a fantasy film concerning black (re)enslavement poorly disguised as a slapstick comedy about a poor adult black man given to a rich white child as a toy. On television, *The Dukes of Hazzard* (1979–1985) repackaged southern segregation with a pair of "good ole boys" racing around Georgia in a 1969 Dodge Charger stock car. The car had a Confederate battle flag painted on the roof and was called the "General Lee," a namesake for Robert E. Lee the commander of the Confederate Army during the Civil War. In case you forgot, Lee fought on the side promoting the perpetuation of black enslavement in America. Lastly, *The Cosby Show* (1984–1992) reveled in the rise of a burgeoning black middle class and signaled the end of racism.[3] Such coded representations promoted subservient black imagery, normalized white racism, and idealized overly assimilationist blacks, a stark reversal of fortune from the unprecedented depictions of militant black folk in 1970s blaxploitation cinema. But oppression, even coded, generates resistance. For example, although the Hollywood Hays Code promoted censorship it also compelled more inventiveness, a point underscored in the following text:

> Producers, directors, and writers were forced to create sex without sex, to produce sexual tension by working around the prohibitions, extending every manner of preliminary to sex. In effect, censorship created plot, and in the process yielded one of the greatest of American film genres: thirties romantic comedy, including the dizzier versions celebrated as screwball comedy. Sex became play—even, at best, a spring like flourishing of fantasy and grace, expressed, most romantically, in the movies of Fred Astaire and Ginger Rogers, in which sex became dance and was transmuted into endless variations on the themes of seduction, submission, revolt, and happiness.[4]

What an ironic twist of creative fate that the racially conservative decade of the 1980s was the cultural catalyst for Prince to put forth unorthodox genre-defining music that was black without being black.

Recall that in the early 1980s, a black group's best chance of breaking into the MTV rotation was getting packaged as a novelty act like the bar band rock group the Bus Boys.[5] Moreover, to assign blame solely to MTV for the racial challenges black artists faced in the 1980s misses the mark and obscures the cultural work that various musical artists such as Prince performed against the reactionary racial politics of the period. As such, during the decade of the 1980s Prince was the Jean-Michel Basquiat of the music industry (or was Basquiat the Prince of the art world?). Either way their neo-expressionism worked to circumvent the racial restraints of the period. For Prince it meant becoming a radical shape-shifter in constant flux, able to engage in a series of racial feints, misdirection, miscues, and surreptitious reaffirmations of his blackness. To this point, Prince created the perfect alchemy of aural and televisual elements that compelled an audience to examine and explore what Prince was about by promoting bisexuality (with songs like "Bambi" and "When You Were Mine") and stylized androgyny. In this sense, the sexual songs and erotic androgynous image of Prince were attuned with the emergent impulses in American popular culture and the increasing infusion of visual eroticism in mainstream music videos.

For example, the British group Duran Duran became a pop phenomenon in America with music videos like "Girls on Film" (1981), a slick video populated with scantily clad attractive women and pretty boy band members. It was pure cotton candy for the eyes of adolescent boys and girls. Accordingly, Prince was in line with the emergent video age of the 1980s whereby sex and sexuality were a central force in attracting interest as an artist. Nevertheless, and for most of his career, Prince performed a racial high-wire act trying to balance mass commercial appeal to an interracial audience with and against his own blackness. Often the contradictions were as synergistic as they were confounding and help to explain how in one decade Prince could pretend to be a biracial, racially ambiguous, sex fiend rock musician, in the next decade a black "gangsta glam" pimp dandy, and settle into a "grown and sexy," racially grounded entertainer and religious proselytizer toward the end of his life. Throughout it all, however, Prince provided a musical body of work that made him a creative visionary in the music industry.

Although the music industry was (and remains to a lesser degree) racially constricted, Prince's music was not; a racially diverse audience of millions of people count themselves as Prince fans, which testifies to Prince's racially transcendent appeal. Fittingly, Prince is a figure that has earned a distinctive place in the American music industry, American popular culture, and the world, a point vividly underscored when the Eiffel Tower, in Paris, France, was bathed in purple light in commemoration of Prince's passing. In the final analysis, whether as listeners, viewing audiences, fans, haters, scholars, casual listeners, or deep-in-the-catalog music enthusiasts, we all have a "Prince" that we consider the "real" Prince. In this sense, Prince is more a cipher for outsiders to project their beliefs, desires, anxieties, and disappointments onto.

But let us not forget the wonder of his music before we become consumed with splitting hairs over the defining version of the man. My own favorite and most definitive "Prince" music springs from the period when Prince was in deep disguise as Jamie Starr making new wave funk-rock on the side. Add to that virtually everything off of *Dirty Mind*, *1999*, and the *Sign o' the Times* releases. In my mind, half of the music from *The Time* was more appropriate for the flip side of the *Dirty Mind* album. Moreover, given that *Dirty Mind* barely clocked in at thirty minutes, the truncated release would have best benefited by having a beefed-up song list. The song order for side two of *Dirty Mind* should have been "Uptown," "Head," "Get It Up," "The Stick," and "Party Up." "Sister," would get axed. At least with this sequence,

Dirty Mind is closer to 50 minutes and with this arrangement the topical thematic of the songs dovetails just right with Prince's sex junkie persona.

Most importantly, given that Prince was an outlier when it came to R&B music of the early 1980s era, the addition of these tracks would have cemented Prince's stature as an R&B auteur instead of an R&B fugitive. In this fashion, Prince could compete right alongside, and on similar ground with, the post-disco grooves of Rick James, the Afrofuturistic funk of Roger Troutman's Zapp band, and the downhome hits of groups like The Gap Band and Maze featuring Frankie Beverly. Unfortunately, for most of the first half of his career, Prince imbued only one track with R&B licks and the type of dance-friendly grooves black folk wanted to hear and possibly purchase. I certainly preferred his more R&B material earlier in his career. I still cherry picked the more R&B-styled songs from his later material up to and including the *Art Official Age* (2014) release that contains my two favorite tracks "Breakdown" and "U Know."

That said, the Prince prior to *Purple Rain* is my favorite "Prince." Having let that "cat out of the bag," I'm sure many of you reading this, if not a majority of you, are mounting an argument as to why I am entirely mistaken. Perhaps there are a few fans out there that have my back and are now breathing a sigh of relief and feel renewed conviction in their taste because I am in perfect agreement with them. Either way, a significant part of the iconic nature of Prince is the stimulating debate he can engender, the sides we take, and how the conclusions we draw from these discussions say less about him and more about us and, by extension, the society we live in. In the end, to paraphrase the late poet Lynn Manning, Prince only waved the wand. We were the magicians.

Acknowledgments

I am grateful to the various people who have provided input and contributed to the completion of this book. Lena Cohen and Sara Shewfelt, former students and research assistants at Loyola Marymount University, did the preparatory groundwork for this project, gathering articles and related material concerning Prince. Thank you to Joe Giannetti, the photographer for the *For You* (1978) album, for his prompt and written retelling of his experience and his take on the experience. Deep bows of appreciation to Nicole Solano, the executive editor at Rutgers University Press, Dayna Hagewood, and all the talented folks at Rutgers University Press for bringing this project to completion.

I must also include a humble and indebted shout-out to my family for having my back while I was deep in the "woodshed."

Prince Rogers Nelson for the music.

Notes

Introduction

1 Allen Beaulieu, *Prince: Before the Rain* (Minnesota Historical Society Press, 2018). In his photographic retrospective of his years as a photographer for Prince, Beaulieu states Prince would stage "candid" shots.

2 Ronin Ro, *Prince: Inside the Music and the Masks* (St. Martin's Press, 2011), 21.

3 Stan Hawkins and Sarah Niblock, *Prince: The Making of a Pop Music Phenomenon* (Routledge, 2011), 9. The authors' claims are problematic, according to the Prince and Dez Dickerson song "Cool," on *The Time* (1981) debut album, which provides a list of what Prince considered cool.

4 John Mundy, *Popular Music On Screen: From Hollywood Musical to Music Video* (Manchester University Press, 1999).

Chapter 1 Incognegro

1 Ronin Ro, *Prince: Inside the Music and the Masks* (St. Martin's Press, 2011), 40.

2 Michaelangelo Matos, Sign 'O' the Times (Continuum: 2015), 34.

3 Andrea Swensson, *Got to Be Something Here: The Rise of the Minneapolis Sound* (University of Minnesota Press, 2017).

4 *Purple Snow: Forecasting the Minneapolis Sound* (2014), 38, 40, 48, 52, 60.

5 Craig Werner, *Higher Ground: Stevie Wonder, Aretha Franklin, Curtis Mayfield, and the Rise and Fall of American Soul* (Crown, 2004).

6 Ro, *Prince*, 28–29.

7 Roger Dean and Storm Thorgerson, *Album Cover Album* (Harper Design, 2008).

8 Tanisha C. Ford, *Liberated Threads: Black Women, Style, and the Global Politics of Soul* (University of North Carolina Press, 2015).

9 Nelson George, "On White Negroes," in *Black on White: Black Writers on What It Means to Be White*, ed. David R. Roediger (Schocken, 1999), 225, 226.

10 Bart Landry, *The New Black Middle Class* (University California Press, 1987).

11 "Midnight TV Show Draws Eyes across Nation," *Billboard*, September 9, 1972, 8.

12 Alice Echols, *Hot Stuff: Disco and the Remaking of American Culture* (W. W. Norton & Company, 2011).

13 Mark Anthony Neal, *Looking for Leroy: Illegible Black Masculinities* (New York University Press: 2013).

14 Matthew Silverman, *Swinging '73: Baseball's Wildest Season* (Rowan & Littlefield, 2013).

15 Claude J. Summers, *The Queer Encyclopedia of Music, Dance, and Musical Theater* (Cleis Press, 2004), 219.

16 Philip Auslander, *Performing Glam Rock: Gender and Theatricality in Popular Music* (University Michigan Press, 2009), 126.

17 Auslander, 149.

18 Alan Light, *Let's Go Crazy* (Atria: 2014), 34.

19 Ken Tucker, "Review: Prince, 'Dirty Mind,'" February 19, 1981. http//www .rollingstone.com/music/albumreviews/dirty-mind.

20 Sam Rubio, "Making It Real," in *New Punk Cinema*, ed. Nicholas Rombes (Edinburgh University Press, 2005), 142; Theo Cateforis, *Are We Not New Wave: Modern Pop at the Turn of the 1980s* (University of Michigan Press, 2014), 24.

21 Jon Savage, *England's Dreaming, Revised Edition: Anarchy, Sex Pistols, Punk Rock, and Beyond* (St. Martin's Griffin, 2002).

22 Ro, *Prince*, 50.

23 Cateforis, *Are We Not New Wave*, 34–35.

24 Ron Becker, Nick Marx, Matt Sienkiewicz, eds., *Saturday Night Live and American TV* (Indiana University Press, 2013), 3.

25 Becker, Marx, Sienkiewicz, 15; Jim Whalle, *Saturday Night Live, Hollywood Comedy, and American Culture: From Chevy Chase to Tina Fey* (Palgrave Macmillan, 2010), 60–61.

26 Cateforis, *Are We Not New Wave*, 86.

27 Geoff Edgers, "The First Time Prince Could Have Saved *Saturday Night Live* from the *Washington Post*," *Washington Post*, October 30, 2014.

28 Bryan Wawzenek, 35 Years Ago: Prince Gets Booed Off the Rolling Stones' Stage, Ultimate Classic Rock, October 8, 2016, http://ultimateclassicrock.com/prince -booed-rolling-stones/.

29 Matt Thorne, *Prince* (Faber & Faber, 2012), 67–68.

30 Heike Jenss, *Fashioning Memory: Vintage Style and Youth Culture* (Bloomsbury, 2015).

Chapter 2 On the Black Hand Side

1 Reebee Garofalo, "Black Popular Music: Crossing Over or Going Under?" in *Rock and Popular Music: Politics, Policies, Institutions*, ed. Tony Bennett et al. (Routledge,1993), 237; Rick Coleman, *Blue Monday: Fats Domino and the Lost Dawn of Rock 'n' Roll* (Da Capo Press, 2007); Richard Campbell, Christopher R. Martin, Bettina Fabos, *Media and Culture: Mass Communication in a Digital Age* (St. Martin's, 2015), 86–87.

2 Jon Fitzgerald, "Motown Crossover Hits 1963–1966 and the Creative Process," *Popular Music* 14, no. 1 (January 1995): 1–11.

3 Gerald Lyn Early, *One Nation Under a Groove: Motown and American Culture* (University of Michigan Press, 2007), 87, 88.

4 Kai Fikentscher, "Disco and House," in *African American Music: An Introduction*, ed. Mellonee V. Burnim and Portia K. Maultsby (Routledge, 2015), 323; Alice Echols, *Hot Stuff: Disco and the Remaking of American Culture* (W. W. Norton & Company, 2011).

5 Echols, 209.

6 Henry Louis Gates, *The Signifying Monkey: A Theory of African-American Literary Criticism* (Oxford University Press, 1988).

7 Nelson George, *The Hippest Trip in America: Soul Train and the Evolution of Culture and Style* (William Morrow, 2014). Prince would make his first in-studio performance in the mid-1990s, well after the show's high-water reign of popularity and relevancy throughout the 1970s into the early 1990s.

8 Matt Thorne, *Prince* (Faber & Faber, 2012), 78.

9 Ronin Ro, *Prince: Inside the Music and the Masks* (St. Martin's Press, 2011), 53.

10 Ro, 67.

11 Ben Greenman, *Dig If You Will the Picture* (Henry, Holt and Co., 2017), 100–103.

12 Ro, *Prince*, 69. In reality she was the wife of Roy Bennett, a production designer on several of Prince's live tours.

13 Debby Miller, "Prince's Hot Rock: The Secret Life of America's Sexiest One-Man Band. What does a twenty-two-year-old musical wizard in bikini briefs have that other rock stars don't? Whatever it is, it makes him the world's sexiest and most influential one-man band," *Rolling Stone*, April 28, 1983.

14 Nelson George, *The Death of Rhythm and Blues* (Penguin Books, 1988), 188.

15 John Mundy, *Popular Music on Screen: From Hollywood Musical to Music Video* (Manchester University Press, 1999).

16 Simon Frith, "Look! Hear! The Uneasy Relationship of Music and Television," *Popular Music* 21, no. 3, Music and Television (October, 2002): 284.

17 John A. Jackson, *A House on Fire: The Rise and Fall of Philadelphia Soul* (Oxford University Press, 2004), 248.

18 Theo Cateforis, *Are We Not New Wave?: Modern Pop at the Turn of the 1980s* (University of Michigan Press, 2011).

19 Dave Rimmer, *New Romantics: The Look* (Omnibus Press, 2013).

20 Rupert Till, *Pop Cult: Religion and Popular Music* (Bloomsbury, 2010), 60; Frenchy Lunning, *Fetish Style* (Bloomsbury Academic, 2013), 48–50; Iain Ellis, *Brit Wits: A History of British Rock Humor* (Intellect, 2012), 101–102.

21 Rickey Vincent, *Funk: The Music, the People, and the Rhythm of the One* (St. Martin's Griffin, 1996), 57.

22 Norman Riley, "Video Wars: A Phenomenon of the Music Industry," *The Crisis* 92, no. 7 (August/September 1985): 27–31; Mike Olszewski, *Radio Daze: Stories from the Front in Cleveland's FM Air Wars* (Kent State University Press, 2003), 189.

23 Tom McGrath, "Integrating MTV," in *Rock and Roll Is Here to Stay: An Anthology*, ed. William McKeen (W. W. Norton & Company, 2000), 459.

24 Rob Tannenbaum and Craig Marks, *I Want My MTV: The Uncensored Story of the Music Revolution* (Plume, 2011), 137–138.

25 Tannenbaum and Marks, 139.

26 Miller, "Prince's Hot Rock."

27 Andrew Flory, *I Hear a Symphony: Motown and Crossover R&B* (University of Michigan Press, 2017), 156.

28 Lisa A. Lewis, *Gender Politics and MTV: Voicing the Difference* (University Temple Press, 1991).

29 Werner Sollors, *Neither Black nor White yet Both: Thematic Explorations of Interracial Literature* (Harvard University Press, 1999).

30 Touré, *I Would Die 4 U: Why Prince Became an Icon* (Audible Studios on Brilliance Audio, 2013); Sollors, 103.

Chapter 3 Enfant Terrible

1 David Farley, "In Minnesota, Celebrating the 30th Anniversary of 'Purple Rain,'" Travel Section, *Los Angeles Times*, July 29, 2014.

2 Allen Light, *Let's Go Crazy: Prince and the Making of Purple Rain* (Atria, 2014), 158.

3 Lisa Taylor, "Baby I'm a Star: Towards a Political Economy of the Actor Formerly Known as Prince," in *Film Stars: Hollywood and Beyond*, ed. Andrew Willis (Manchester University Press, 2004), 158–173.

4 Donald Bogle, *Toms, Coons, Mulattoes, Mammies, and Bucks: An Interpretive History of Blacks in American Films* (Bloomsbury Academic, 2015), 290.

5 Eric Lott, *Love and Theft: Blackface Minstrelsy and the American Working Class* (Oxford University Press, 1993).

6 Karen L. Cox, *Dreaming of Dixie: How the South Was Created in American Popular Culture* (University of North Carolina Press, 2013), 98–99.

7 Bogle, *Toms, Coons, Mulattoes*, 119, 121.

8 Amanda Howell, *Popular Film Music and Masculinity in Action: A Different Tune* (Routledge, 2015), 74–75.

9 Although The Revolution has a black member of the band who performs upstage and alongside The Kid he is virtually absent from *Purple Rain*. Moreover, all the white band members have speaking lines in the film except for him. In contrast, Wendy, the white female guitarist, garners the most screen time when The Kid performs onstage. Without a doubt, The Kid and Wendy exude personal chemistry in the film. As a consequence, a reasonable explanation for her lopsided screen time relative to the black member of the group is the personal chemistry that she and Prince share as musicians when they are performing, a quality that has nothing to do with purposefully upholding a racial message.

10 Stan Hawkins and Sarah Niblock, *Prince: The Making of a Pop Music Phenomenon* (Ashgate, 2011), 104.

11 The aloof sketch became a signature image in the video "When Doves Cry." The kaleidoscopic special effects portion of the video recycles the image as a wall-size backdrop for the entire band.

12 Hawkins and Niblock, *Prince*.

13 "The Kid in particular is excessively feminized in his clothing, hair and make-up, an external signifier of his internal struggle to reconcile his femininity with his masculinity. Ultimately it is the power of the mother object which enables him to embrace his inner femininity to help him forge positive non-patriarchal relationships with the women in his social sphere." Hawkins and Niblock, *Prince*, 103.

14 "Excerpt: Places in The Heart / Purple Rain" in *New Position: The Prince Chronicles* (Resistance Works, 2016), 17–22.

15 Nelson George, *The Death of Rhythm and Blues* (Penguin Books, 1988), 188.

16 Taylor, "Baby I'm a Star," 165.

17 Henry Louis Gates Jr., *The Signifying Monkey: A Theory of African American Literary Criticism* (Oxford University Press, 1989).

18 Simon Price, "Cult Heroes: Morris Day—*Purple Rain* Rival Who Almost Stole Prince's Thunder," *Guardian*, April 26, 2016.

19 *TOP POP: Apollonia 6*, "Sex Shooter," aired September 22, 1984, https://youtu.be /VGaMIGmwyfY.

20 Robert Palmer, "Prince's 'Around The World'" *New York Times*, April 22, 1985.

21 "Raspberry Beret" reached #2 on the *Billboard* Hot 100, and "Pop Life" reached number 7 on the US *Billboard* Hot 100 Chart.

22 Matt Thorne, *Prince* (Faber & Faber, 2012).

23 Ronin Ro, *Prince: Inside the Music and the Masks* (St. Martin's Press, 2011), 133.

24 Ro, 115, 116.

25 Lynn Norment, "Prince: What Is the Secret of His Amazing Success?" *Ebony*, June 1985, 166.

26 Bill Brown, *You Should've Heard Just What I Seen: Collected Newspaper Articles, 1981–1984* (Colossal Books, 2010), 69, 70.

27 Ro, *Prince*, 115.

28 Griffin Woodworth, "Prince, Miles, and Maceo: Horns, Masculinity, and the Anxiety of Influence," *Black Music Research Journal* 33, no. 2 (Fall 2013): 119.

29 "Rick James: The Untold Story" *Vibe*, April 1994, 52–55.

Chapter 4 Cherry Bomb

1 Sumiko Higashi, *Stars, Fans, and Consumption in the 1950s: Reading Photoplay* (Palgrave, 2016).

2 Chris Rojek, *Fame Attack: The Inflation of Celebrity and Its Consequences* (Bloomsbury Academic, 2012), 96–97.

3 David T. Friendly, "Prince for a Day in Wyoming," First Look at the Studios, *Los Angeles Times*, July 3, 1986.

4 John Rockwell, "Prince's 'Parade' Stakes a Claim to Popularity," Arts Section, *New York Times*, March 30, 1986.

5 Friendly, "Prince for a Day."

6 Stan Hawkins and Sarah Niblock, *Prince: The Making of a Pop Music Phenomenon* (Routledge, 2012), 70.

7 Lisa Taylor, "Baby I'm a Star: Towards a Political Economy of the Actor Formerly Known as Prince," in *Film Stars: Hollywood and Beyond*, ed. Andrew Willis (Manchester University Press, 2004), 172.

8 Saverio Giovacchini and Robert Sklar, eds. *Global Neorealism: The Transnational History of a Film Style* (University of Mississippi Press, 2012).

9 Walter Goodman, "*Under the Cherry Moon* (1986) Screen: Prince in 'Cherry Moon,'" *New York Times*, July 3, 1986; Keith Corson, *Trying to Get Over: African American Directors after Blaxploitation, 1977–1986* (University Texas Press, 2016).

10 Tyler Stoval, *Paris Noir: African American in the City of Light* (Houghton Mifflin, 1996).

11 Corson, *Trying to Get Over*, 194.

12 Mark Anthony Neal, *Soul Babies: Black Popular Culture and the Post-Soul Aesthetic* (Routledge, 2001).

13 Taylor, "Baby I'm a Star," 164, 172.

14 Donald Bogle, *Toms, Coons, Mulattoes, Mammies, and Bucks: An Interpretive History of Blacks in American Films* (Bloomsbury Academic, 2015).

15 Randy Shilts, *And the Band Played On: Politics, People, and the AIDS Epidemic* (Penguin Books, 1988).

16 Matt Thorne, *Prince* (Faber & Faber: 2012), 130.

17 Corson, *Trying to Get Over*, 189.

18 Ronin Ro, *Prince: Inside the Music and the Masks* (St. Martin's Press, 2011), 139, 140, 156–160.

19 Daniel Kreps, "Aretha Franklin Bans 'Amazing Grace' Doc Screenings 1972 Documentary about Recording of Classic Live LP Barred from Premiering at Telluride Film Festival," *Rolling Stone*, September 5, 2015.

20 Ro, *Prince*, 164.

21 Ro, 158.

22 Thorne, *Prince*, 187.

23 Ronin Ro, 116.

24 B. Gottschild, *The Black Dancing Body: A Geography from Coon to Cool* (Palgrave Macmillan, 2005).

25 Craig Hansen Werner, *A Change Is Gonna Come: Music, Race and the Soul of America* (University of Michigan Press, 2006).

26 *Jet* (March 25, 1985), 61.

27 John Gennari, "Miles and the Jazz Critics," by John Gennari in *Miles Davis and American Culture*, ed. Gerald Lyn Early (Missouri Historical Society Press, 2001), 67–77.

28 Quincy Troup, *Miles: The Autobiography* (Simon and Schuster, 1989), 360–361.

29 Stanley Crouch, *Considering Genius: Writings on Jazz* (Basic Civitas, 2007), 240.

30 Ro, *Prince*, 172.

31 Stan Beeler, *Dance, Drugs, and Escape: The Club Scene in Literature, Film and Television since the Late 1980s* (McFarland & Company, 2007), 88–91.

32 Bob Gulla, ed., *Icons of R&B and Soul: An Encyclopedia of the Artists Who Revolutionized Rhythm, Volume 2* (Greenwood, 2007), 494.

33 Thorne, *Prince* (Faber & Faber, 2012), 202, 203; Touré, *I Would Die 4 U: Why Prince Became an Icon* (Atria Books: 2013), 135.

34 Simon Reynolds, *Energy Flash: A Journey through Rave Music and Dance Culture* (Soft Skull Press, 2012).

35 Simon Firth, "What Is Bad Music," in *Bad Music: The Music We Love to Hate*, ed. Christopher Washburne and Maiken Derno (Routledge, 2004), 15–37.

36 Mark Anthony Neal, *Looking for Leroy: Illegible Black Masculinities* (New York University Press, 2013), 53.

Chapter 5 Chaos and Crossroads

1 Joseph Vogel, *This Thing Called Life: Prince, Race, Sex, Religion, and Music* (Bloomsbury Academic, 2018), 117.

2 Jeff Chang, *Total Chaos: The Art and Aesthetics of Hip-Hop* (Civitas Books, 2007).

3 Reiland Rabaka, *Hip Hop's Inheritance: From the Harlem Renaissance to the Hip Hop Feminist* (Lexington Books, 2011), 66.

4 Vogel, *This Thing Called Life*, 84.

5 Jeffrey A. Brown, *The Modern Superhero in Film and Television: Popular Genre and American Culture* (Routledge, 2016), 17–18.

6 Armond White, *New Position: The Prince Chronicles* (Resistance Works, 2016), 85–91.

7 Eileen R. Meehan, "'Holy Commodity Fetish, Batman!': The Political Economy of a Commercial Intertext," in *Many More Lives of the Batman*, ed. Roberta Pearson, William Uricchio, and Will Brooker (British Film Institute, 2015), 69–70.

8 *Spin Magazine*, July 2005, 70; Michaelangelo Matos, *Prince's Sign o' the Times*, Thirty Three and a Third series. (Bloomsbury Academic, 2004).

9 Jonathan Markovitz, *Legacies of Lynching: Racial Violence and Memory* (University of Minnesota Press, 2004).

10 Ronin Ro, *Prince: Inside the Music and the Masks* (St. Martin's Press, 2011), 210.

11 "Prince Donates Proceeds from New Song to UNCF" *Jet*, March 23, 1992, 21.

12 Frank Kofsky, *Black Music, White Business: Illuminating the History and Political Economy of Jazz* (Pathfinder Press, 1998).

13 Edward Royce, *The Origins of Southern Sharecropping* (Temple University Press, 1993).

14 Thorne views this album as a punk-rock equivalent to Gayes's *Here, My Dear*. History has not supported such a supposition. The album remains out of print.

15 Matt Thorne, *Prince*, (Faber & Faber: 2012) 310.

16 David Ritz, *Divided Soul: The Life of Marvin Gaye* (Da Capo Press, 1985), 234.

17 Michael Eric Dyson, *Mercy, Mercy Me: The Art, Loves and Demons of Marvin Gaye* (Basic Civitas Books, 2008), 231.

18 Jim Irvin, *The MOJO Collection: The Ultimate Music Companion* (Canongate Books Ltd., 2007), 416.

19 Wynton Marsalis, "Premature Autopsies (Sermon)," in *Majesty of the Blues* (Columbia Records: 1989). Sermon delivered by Reverend Jeremiah Wright Jr.

20 Sacha Jenkins, "The Real Thing: D'Angelo Listens Back—and Fans Hear History in the Making," *Vibe*, September, 1996, 106–108.

21 Datwon Thomas, "This Is an A/B Conversation," *Vibe*, March 2000, 210; , *Spin Magazine*, "100 Greatest Albums 1985–2005" July 2005, 90.

22 Stanley Crouch, *The All-American Skin Game, or Decoy of Race: The Long and the Short of It* (Vintage, 1997).

23 Greg Tate, "Miles in the 1980s," in *Miles Davis: The Complete Illustrated History*, ed. Ron Carter et al. (Voyageur Press, 2012), 206.

24 "Questlove Remembers Prince: In This Life, You're on Your Own: In a powerful essay, the Roots leader goes deep on the genius, loneliness and the secret hip-hop heart of his idol," *Rolling Stone*, April 25, 2016, http://www.rollingstone.com/music/news/questlove-remembers-prince-in-this-life-youre-on-your-own.

25 Touré, *Never Drank the Kool-Aide* (Picador, 2006), 266.

26 William Jelani Cobb, *The Devil and Dave Chappelle: And Other Essays* (Basic Books, 2007), 248.

27 Given how Prince and Rick James were at one time creative foils for one another it is fitting that Chappelle would also reenact Rick James in a separate skit drawing on the Hollywood lore surrounding Rick James's lifestyle. The skit was a double-edged sword. It reinvigorated the popularity of Rick James's personality and past exploits more than his impressive catalog of music he created early in his career.

28 James J. Donahue, "Charlie Murphy: American Storyteller," in *Post-Soul Satire: Black Identity after Civil Rights*, ed. Derek C. Maus and James J. Donahue (University of Mississippi Press, 2014), 229.

Chapter 6 Don't Call It a Comeback ...

1 Judy Kutulas, *After Aquarius Dawned: How the Revolutions of the Sixties Became the Popular Culture of the Seventies* (North Carolina Press, 2017).
2 Craig Werner, *Higher Ground* (Three River Press, 2004), 198, 199, 230.
3 Touré, *I Would Die 4 U: Why Prince Became an Icon* (Atria Books: 2013).
4 Mireille Miller-Young, *A Taste of Brown Sugar: Black Women in Pornography* (Duke University Press, 2014).
5 Ken Mansfield and Marshall Terrill, *Rock and a Heart Place: A Rock 'n' Roller-Coaster Ride from Rebellion to Sweet Salvation* (Broadstreet Publishing Group, 2015); Hyun Kim, "Blessed the Child," interview, *Vibe*, July 2003, 62.
6 Matt Thorne, Prince, (Faber&Faber: 2012), 394.
7 Las Vegas Weekly Staff, "The 25 Greatest Headliners in Las Vegas History," *Las Vegas Weekly*, December 13, 2012,
8 Frantz Fanon, *Black Skins, White Masks* (Grove Press, 1967), 129–131.
9 Touré, *I Would Die 4 U*, 104.
10 *The Last "Darky": Bert Williams, Black-on-Black Minstrelsy, and the African Diaspora* (Duke University Press: 2006), 125.
11 John Gennari, *Blowin' Hot and Cool: Jazz and Its Critics* (University of Chicago Press, 2006), 317.
12 John Szwed, *See So What: The Life of Miles Davis* (Simon & Schuster, 2004), 196.
13 Alan Light, *Let's Go Crazy: Prince and the Making of* Purple Rain (Atria Books, 2014), 231–234.
14 Ben Greenman, *Dig If You Will the Picture: Funk, Sex, God and Genius in the Music of Prince* (Henry Holt, 2017), 152–154.
15 Yvonne Wenger, "Thousands Turn Out for Prince's 'Rally 4 Peace' Benefit Concert," *Baltimore Sun*, May 10, 2015.
16 James Sullivan, *The Hardest Working Man: How James Brown Saved the Soul of America* (Gotham, 2008).
17 Matt Thorne, *Prince*, (Faber&Faber: 2012), 366–377.

Chapter 7 Dearly Beloved: An Epitath

1 Spencer Kornhaber, "The Noble Futility of Madonna's Prince Tribute," *Atlantic*, May 23, 2016, http://www.theatlantic.com/entertainment/archive/2016/05/madonna-prince-billboard-awards-tribute-criticism-bet/483893/.
2 Ian Haney Lopez, *Dog Whistle Politics: How Coded Racial Appeals Have Reinvented Racism and Wrecked the Middle Class* (Oxford University Press, 2014).
3 Willian J. Wilson, *The Declining Significance of Race: Blacks and Changing American Institutions* (University of Chicago Press, 1978).
4 David Denby, "Sex and Sexier: The Hays Code Wasn't All Bad," Section A, *New Yorker*, May 2, 2016.
5 *Soul: The Definitive Guide to R&B Soul* (Backbeat: 2002), 102.

Index

About the Author

ADILIFU NAMA is a professor of African American studies at Loyola Marymount University in Los Angeles, California, and the author of the award-winning titles *Race on the QT: Blackness and the Films of Quentin Tarantino*, *Super Black: American Pop Culture and Black Superheroes*, and *Black Space: Imagining Race in Science Fiction Film*.